CHAMPA BAY!

THE TAMPA BAY BUCCANEERS'
UNFORGETTABLE 2020 CHAMPIONSHIP SEASON

T0159332

This book is available in quantity at special discounts for your group or organization. For further information, contact:

Triumph Books LLC
814 North Franklin Street
Chicago, Illinois 60610
Phone: (312) 337-0747
www.triumphbooks.com

Printed in U.S.A.
ISBN: 978-1-62937-909-8

Content packaged by Mojo Media, Inc.
Joe Funk: Editor
Jason Hinman: Creative Director

Front and back cover photos by AP Images

All interior photos by AP Images

CONTENTS

FOREWORD

By Rondé Barber

When the Bucs drafted me in 1997, I can honestly say I knew very little about Tampa. I had only been to Florida a couple of times in college for games, and I'm not sure I even knew where exactly Tampa was located in the state.

But it didn't take me long to realize that Tampa is a pretty unique and special place. Look, we're talking about 4 million people in the Tampa Bay area, so it has almost everything you'd want in a big city. The beauty of Tampa, however, is how it's really more like a small town. It's very easy-going, friendly and welcoming, and you feel like you know everyone.

I actually told Tom Brady this when he signed with the Bucs. I knew he would love it here, too. Tom is arguably the greatest quarterback of all time, so I was very optimistic about the team becoming a contender, especially when coupled with Bruce Arians, who in his second year has redefined this organization.

But a trip to the Super Bowl in their first year together? And a Super Bowl win, at that? Who really could have expected this? To be legendary, you must do legendary things. To win the ultimate game, you must capture your moment.

We just witnessed history. The Bucs won a Super Bowl played at Raymond James Stadium in Tampa. Let that sink in. We're a championship town again, with the Lightning winning the Stanley Cup and the Rays nearly winning the World Series. What a special time for all the fans.

I am one of those fans because I have so much invested in the emotional bank account after playing here for 16 years. The Bucs owners and everyone in the building have always treated me like family, so I am, and always will be, a Buc for life.

Of course, there were some rough years. It's gut-wrenching to watch your team repeatedly struggle

and lose. You almost feel like a big brother to the guys, sharing their passion for both success and devastation in bad results. You want it for them that badly, that same special feeling you once had as a Super Bowl champion.

No team was more special to me than our 2002 Bucs. It was such a magical time. When you win a Super Bowl, it puts an exclamation point on not only the season but your entire career. All your work finally has paid off. Your team is immortalized. No matter who you are, what team you're on or what position you play, the goal is always to win the Super Bowl. Always. That's why you play.

Every single year, you hope you've done enough to be the best at your craft. It was validation to win a Super Bowl, and I'd hate to think what my career would be without that.

So many great players never get that moment — my brother, Tiki, being one of them — and there's such an emptiness to get that far and come up short. You're so happy for the players who can enjoy a championship. Besides getting married and having kids, I've never had a moment quite like that. It was overwhelming.

But even as overwhelming as winning a Super Bowl can be, it's really all about the journey; about all the little things that really define you — the ups and downs, and the celebration of all those experiences with your teammates. You never lose that — ever.

I saw incredible resiliency from these Bucs. They had times when they started slowly and seemed to be chasing everything and nothing all at the same time. They had moments when people doubted them. They were 7-5, and then went 7-0 as everything came together down the stretch.

This was a team built through the draft, supplemented with some great free agency decisions. As the season progressed, I saw great balance, where they didn't have to rely solely on any one person or unit. The running game really contributed. The defense played great

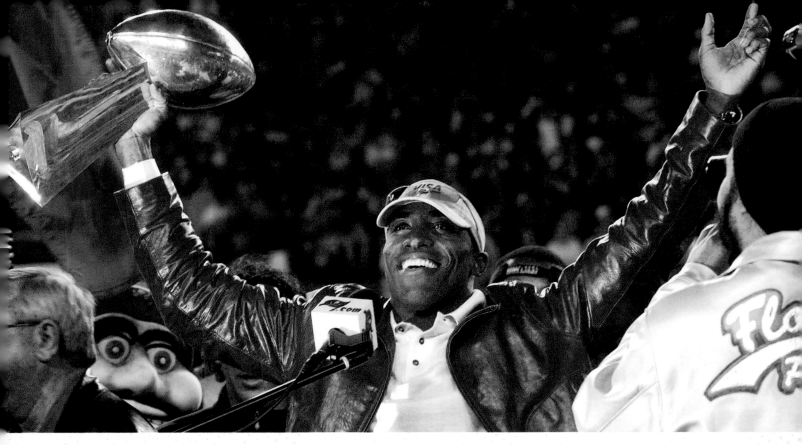

Ronde Barber waves the Vince Lombardi Trophy during the celebration following the Buccaneers' victory over the Raiders in Super Bowl XXXVII. Barber knows firsthand not only the hard work that goes into a Super Bowl championship, but also the elation after you accomplish your goal.

by stopping the run like always, but also by taking the ball away and creating huge turnovers that decided games.

Of course, we have to talk about Tom Brady. I only played against him a couple of times, but I remember feeling pretty helpless. It wasn't that we were that bad. It's just that he was that good. He's an above-the-neck type of player. He transformed this team with his attitude and his approach to the game.

I can't comprehend that he's 43 and still doing this. With everything he had already won and accomplished in his career, he still wanted more. He has an internal drive most people can't even fathom. But I honestly think that mindset rubbed off on every single member of the Bucs organization and really influenced the players who hadn't had much success before his arrival.

It's hard to believe one guy has seven Super Bowl rings. It's funny, but I never bring out my Super Bowl ring. If somebody specifically asks to see it, I'll dig it out of the safe, but I don't really have any big mementos. The Super Bowl is more about the memories, the little snippets of history, the journey itself — all those little moments that add up to a championship football team. Now our community has those moments and

memories to enjoy once again. It was so rewarding to see our team raise another Lombardi Trophy. Amidst a global pandemic, it has been incredible to watch our community enjoy this ultimate triumph. It was a special win from a special team for a special town.

I'm so happy for the Bucs and all of Tampa Bay. Our team, our town, our moment. ∎

Rondé Barber, a Pro Football Hall of Fame finalist and Buccaneers Ring of Honor member, played 16 seasons at defensive back (1997-2012) for the Bucs. He was a five-time Pro Bowler, a three-time first-team All-Pro and a member of the NFL 2000s All-Decade Team. He's the NFL record-holder for most consecutive starts at defensive back (224, including playoffs). Barber is the only NFL player ever to record a career 45 interceptions and 25 sacks. He owns the signature play in franchise history (92-yard interception return in the NFC Championship Game that sent the 2002 Bucs to Super Bowl XXXVII). Off the field, Barber is Vice-Chair of Copperhead Charities, host organization for the Valspar Championship, and has co-written 13 children's books with his twin brother, Tiki.

INTRODUCTION

Nine days before Super Bowl LV in Tampa, Buccaneers owner/co-chairman Bryan Glazer spoke at an introductory news conference.

"If you walked up to someone in this community three years ago when we were awarded this Super Bowl originally and you said to them, 'The Tampa Bay Buccaneers would be playing in this game and Tom Brady would be your quarterback,' they would just think you're insane," Glazer said.

"And yet, here we are on the cusp of something unbelievable."

We have seen a lot through 45 seasons of Buccaneer football.

Now we have witnessed something truly unbelievable.

Bruce Arians' Bucs are Super Bowl winners … after defeating the defending champion Kansas City Chiefs … at Tampa's Raymond James Stadium … with Tom Brady at quarterback.

Take a minute to absorb that.

Oh, and all this after playing the entire NFL season during a pandemic, which required unprecedented testing and precautions, along with performing before a sparse gathering of fans (or, in some stadiums, no crowd at all).

The Bucs ended a 12-season playoff drought, which seems like a lot. Until you consider that the franchise went from 1983-96 (14 seasons) without a winning record. And that doesn't even mention the fact that the expansion Bucs lost their first 26 games before tasting victory.

You can't make this stuff up.

Inaugural coach John McKay once was asked what he thought of his team's execution.

"I'm in favor of it," McKay said.

You needed a laugh track back then. The Bucs banished three quarterbacks — Doug Williams, Steve Young and Trent Dilfer — who wound up leading other teams to Super Bowl titles. They used the draft's overall No. 1 pick for Heisman Trophy-winning running back Bo Jackson, who promptly opted for baseball.

Things got better, but there were times when we wondered if the Bucs would reach the Super Bowl in our lifetime.

That all changed in 2002, when Jon Gruden's Bucs beat the nemesis Philadelphia Eagles in the NFC Championship Game, then smashed the Oakland Raiders in Super Bowl XXXVII at San Diego. It was an all-time defense and an opportunistic offense. Afterward, we saw the team's general manager dancing with the Lombardi Trophy. There were parades and banquets and an offseason with nonstop basking.

We thought it could be a dynasty, but that didn't happen.

The Bucs promptly went through 17 consecutive seasons without a playoff victory. There were five different head coaches and 13 different starting quarterbacks during that span. At times, it was bleak.

Even when times were especially bad, we still had our once-in-a-lifetime moment.

It almost sounded like a fairy tale: Once upon a time, kids, the Bucs won the Super Bowl.

And now?

Bucs winning the Super Bowl again? Hey, it's a twice-in-a-lifetime moment.

We looked it up. The Bucs now have more Super Bowl titles than 18 franchises, including 13 that already were in place (Bears, Bengals, Bills, Cardinals, Chargers, Eagles, Falcons, Jets, Lions, Rams, Saints, Titans and Vikings) when the expansion Bucs arrived in 1976.

The Bucs have two Lombardi Trophies, as many as

Tom Brady and the Bucs captured the second Super Bowl title in franchise history, fulfilling the promise of a roster put together with championship aspirations.

the Colts, Chiefs, Dolphins and Ravens. In fact, only nine franchises have more Super Bowl titles than the Bucs.

Who could have imagined it?

And who could have imagined Brady's bunch? The Greatest of All Time in Tampa Bay? It happened. Rob Gronkowski, Antonio Brown and Leonard Fournette happened, too. The Bucs developed a stout, ball-hawking defense. There was no more cringing on field-goal or extra-point attempts.

It was a great team for a great setting. Tampa Bay hosted its fifth Super Bowl. The pandemic complicated matters for organizers, who were robbed of maximum economic impact, packed hotels and full airline flights.

It was a different scene for the Super Bowl. Very different. This time, the home team was there. And local enthusiasm was off the charts.

It was a week for all of Tampa Bay to shine. Fittingly, on Super Bowl Eve, former Bucs safety John Lynch was selected for the Pro Football Hall of Fame. Lynch will join Lee Roy Selmon, Warren Sapp, Derrick Brooks and Coach Tony Dungy in Canton.

All of that — and a Bucs' Super Bowl victory in Tampa?

As Bryan Glazer said: Unbelievable.

We hope you enjoy looking back at a championship season that none of us will ever forget. ∎

— *Greg Auman and Joey Johnston*

SUPER BOWL LV

BUCCANEERS 31, CHIEFS 9
February 7, 2021 • Tampa, Florida

FIRE THE CANNONS!

Bucs Capture Super Bowl in Season Like No Other

By Greg Auman

If the very idea of Tom Brady starting a new chapter in his storied career with the Tampa Bay Buccaneers was incredible to begin with, then what can you say about the 43-year-old winning a Super Bowl championship with his new team on their own home field?

Brady said it would be "a magical season," and it was never more magical than Feb. 7, when the Bucs beat the defending champion Kansas City Chiefs in resounding fashion, rolling to a 31-9 victory at Raymond James Stadium for the franchise's second-ever title.

"We came together at the right time," said Brady, who threw three touchdown passes in the Super Bowl win, giving him an even 50 for the entire 20-game run to a championship. "Every year is amazing. This team is world champions forever. You can't take it away from us."

NFL commissioner Roger Goodell, in presenting the Lombardi Trophy after the game, summed up well the convergence of Tampa's Super Bowl coming on their home field in the middle of a pandemic.

"In a season we will never forget, you are the Super Bowl champions we will always remember," he said. "The Vince Lombardi Trophy is staying in Tampa Bay."

Just 10 weeks earlier, the Bucs didn't look like champions. The same Chiefs team had jumped out to a 17-0 lead on the way to a 27-24 victory that left the Bucs at 7-5, barely in the playoffs as a wild card. But after a much-needed bye week, coach Bruce Arians and the Bucs finished the regular season with four straight wins, then built on that momentum in the postseason with three road playoff wins to set up the ultimate home game in Super Bowl LV.

Brady throwing three touchdowns, two to tight end Rob Gronkowski, you might expect that in a Super Bowl. But what was most impressive was a Bucs defense rising up for the third straight game to beat a former Super Bowl MVP quarterback. They got three interceptions against the Saints' Drew Brees, they went into Lambeau Field and eliminated the 2020 league MVP in Aaron Rodgers, but the best performance of all came in shutting down Chiefs quarterback Patrick Mahomes.

"They stepped up to the challenge," Brady said of his defense, which held the Chiefs to single-digit scoring for the first time in 54 games with Mahomes at quarterback. "You go up against a guy like Pat, an incredible player, and Aaron, an MVP, two weeks ago they played incredible, (against) Drew, they played great. They stepped up. They rose to the occasion. We

Tight end Rob Gronkowski was in prime form in Super Bowl LV, with six catches for 67 yards and two pivotal touchdowns.

needed it, playing extremely talented offenses, but I'm so happy we all came to play tonight."

Defensive coordinator Todd Bowles had seen Mahomes throw for 462 yards in the first meeting, but his defense came into the game with confidence, having won in rematches in each of their last two playoff games. The Bucs pressured Mahomes, held him to field goals instead of touchdowns, then closed out the game with two interceptions to complete a dominating finish to their season.

"It's amazing," linebacker Lavonte David said of winning a championship after missing the playoffs in each of his first eight seasons in Tampa. "We knew we were doubted. We knew we could play football with these guys. You take your hat off to them. They're a great football team. But we knew we had a great football team, too. The feeling in this locker room is incredible. Guys are jumping for joy. It's a great feeling. I'm glad I'm celebrating with the great group of guys we have. We're going to be forever remembered."

And while the defense stepped up in those final three wins, having Brady at quarterback instilled a new confidence in the Bucs. Even though the Bucs hadn't made the playoffs in 13 years, their new leader had a history of nothing but postseason success, one that permeated the entire locker room over the course of a season.

While the defense kept Mahomes in check, holding him to the lowest-rated game of his NFL career, Brady stepped up, his 125.8 quarterback rating his highest in any of his 10 Super Bowls. He threw three touchdowns to lead the Bucs to a 21-6 halftime lead, the last a stunner, much like the Bucs had pulled off before halftime in Green Bay.

They got the ball at their 29 with 55 seconds and no time outs, the big play coming when Brady threw a deep pass to Mike Evans, incomplete but resulting in a 34-yard pass interference penalty. Another pass put them at the 9-yard line with 13 seconds to go, then another pass-interference penalty drawn by Evans put them at the 1-yard line, and Brady connected with

Running back Leonard Fournette (28) made a major impact throughout the win, gaining 89 yards and a touchdown on 16 carries and adding four catches and 46 yards through the air.

Linebacker Shaquil Barrett (58) and the Bucs' defense made life extremely difficult on Patrick Mahomes (15) and the Kansas City offense, pressuring Mahomes a Super bowl record 29 times and holding the Chiefs to single-digits in scoring for the first time in the quarterback's career.

receiver Antonio Brown to help separate Tampa Bay from the defending champs.

From there on, the defense wouldn't let the Chiefs threaten at all, allowing players the chance to celebrate the last hour of a victory while it was still happening on the field. A socially distanced crowd of 25,000, including some 7,500 vaccinated health-care workers there as guests of the league as a thank-you for their hard work and sacrifice, saw a victory that exceeded all expectations.

Arians, in his first Super Bowl as a head coach at age 68, deflected the praise to his assistants and his team, saying they executed at a high level all season, especially in the final push to a memorable championship.

"This one belongs to our coaching staff and our players," Arians said. "This is your trophy. I didn't do a damn thing. You guys won this game, you came together as a band of brothers and you made it happen. I'm so proud of all of you." ∎

Above: In his second year with Tampa Bay, Bruce Arians became the oldest coach to win a Super Bowl in NFL history, at 68 years and 127 days. Opposite: Safety Antoine Winfield Jr. celebrates a third quarter interception, one of two on the day for the Tampa Bay defense.

Linebacker Devin White (45) spearheaded a relentless Bucs' defensive attack, piling up a game-leading 12 tackles, including two tackles for loss.

TOMPA BAY

Brady Earns Super Bowl MVP with Confident Performance

By Joey Johnston

Tompa Bay, anyone?

It began as a joke from Tampa mayor Jane Castor. If Tom Brady, 43, could lead the Buccaneers to victory at Super Bowl LV — at the team's home field of Raymond James Stadium, no less — well, maybe it would be appropriate for the Tampa Bay region to rename itself.

Castor was joking, right?

We're not sure.

Because Brady, the former New England Patriots quarterback who was the catalyst of the Bucs' championship transformation, entered another dimension when Tampa Bay deflated the Kansas City Chiefs 31-9.

Brady, who completed 21 of 29 passes for 201 yards and three touchdowns, was selected Most Valuable Player even though his statistics weren't necessarily overwhelming. But the subtleties of Tampa Bay's performance — Brady's ability to utilize his weapons and avoid game-altering mistakes — again spotlighted why his presence elevated the Bucs to a title-deserving franchise.

That was his value.

"My father (Malcolm Glazer) had a saying," Bucs owner and co-chairman Joel Glazer said. "You want to know the road ahead? Ask the person who has been there."

Brady has been there before — over and over again.

He's the first seven-time Super Bowl champion, and he now has more titles by himself than the Patriots and Pittsburgh Steelers franchises (six each).

He's the first player to win a Super Bowl title in three different decades.

Plus, as a three-time Super Bowl MVP and seven-time champion, he has entered rarefied air encompassing all major American sports. He can be compared to Bill Russell (11 NBA titles, five MVPs); Yogi Berra (10 World Series titles, three MVPs); Joe DiMaggio (nine World Series titles, three MVPs); and Mickey Mantle (seven World Series titles, three MVPs).

But this season was different. In the COVID-19 era, there were no formal offseason workouts, no exhibition games and very little time to acclimate to new surroundings after 20 seasons in New England.

Still, Brady didn't miss a beat, even when the Bucs were 7-5 after losing against the Chiefs in the regular season. The Bucs closed it out with eight straight victories and became the first team in NFL history to score 30 or more points in four consecutive postseason games.

"I loved experiencing a championship with this group of guys," Brady sad. "This team is a world champion forever."

The Bucs were 7-9 in 2019 — close to postseason contention, but not close enough. The team had talent. Brady taught the Bucs how to win.

"When we got Tom, I knew it (winning the Super Bowl) was a possibility," Bucs wide receiver Mike Evans said. "The past wasn't too nice. Early exits every year. I was having Super Bowl parties at my house, at the crib, and now I'm competing in the game.

"When Tom came, I learned how to take care of my body better, how to study film better, how to become a better man. He's a great role model. He's the greatest of all time." ■

Tom Brady further cemented his case as the greatest quarterback in NFL history, winning his seventh Super Bowl championship and third Super Bowl MVP in his iconic career.

PERFECT TIMING

General Manager Jason Licht Combines Measured Roster Construction with Big Offseason Acquisitions for Super Results

By Greg Auman

Jason Licht was building a championship roster long before he talked Tom Brady into coming to Tampa.

Landing a six-time Super Bowl champion can go a long way toward accelerating a franchise's return to relevance, but the Bucs' long path to a Super Bowl appearance started seven years earlier, when Licht took over as general manager.

"My first pick!" Licht shouted in greeting and embracing receiver Mike Evans at Lambeau Field in the minutes after Tampa Bay's NFC Championship Game victory over the Packers.

Licht had the good sense with the No. 7 pick that first year to take Evans and not his quarterback at Texas A&M, Johnny Manziel, and the receiver has topped 1,000 receiving yards in each of his first seven seasons, an NFL record. His next draft netted two starting offensive linemen in Donovan Smith and Ali Marpet, and while he hasn't hit on every high pick, he's built a team that can win now but also well beyond the 2020 season.

"I'm very humbled," he said three days after the Bucs advanced to the Super Bowl. "Once again, I use the word 'grateful.' I knew that I had a special staff. I knew that with BA (Bruce Arians), we had a rare coach ... we have a rare coaching staff. Just for it to finally come together the way it did this year, so far, it's a humbling experience."

Landing Brady in March was a huge swing, and Licht had come up in two separate stints in the Patriots front office, so he knew well the leadership that Brady would bring to a team that hadn't made the playoffs since 2007. The Bucs had set team scoring records in Arians' first season in 2019, but quarterback Jameis Winston couldn't solve a turnover problem, throwing 30 interceptions and losing five fumbles, making consistent winning more difficult.

After signing Brady to a two-year, $50 million deal, the Bucs sent a fourth-round pick to the Patriots for the rights to tight end Rob Gronkowski, who came out of retirement and caught seven touchdown passes in his first Bucs season, reuniting with his quarterback. Other key offensive weapons, like running back Leonard Fournette and receiver Antonio Brown, would join an already loaded offense to build around Brady. To help protect their 43-year-old quarterback, he used his top draft pick on Iowa tackle Tristan Wirfs, who played every snap all season as the team's right tackle.

Licht's evaluation skills can be seen all over the Bucs' roster — super signings like outside linebacker Shaquil Barrett, who led the NFL with 19.5 sacks in 2019, or trades like the one for pass-rusher Jason Pierre-Paul, another key part of Tampa Bay's defense. That defense was built through the draft, getting three starters by trading one pick in 2018 to land defensive tackle Vita Vea, cornerback Carlton Davis and safety Jordan Whitehead. The next draft brought linebacker

---

Tight end Rob Gronkowski was one of the major offseason additions for general manager Jason Licht and the Buccaneers.

Devin White and corners Jamel Dean and Sean Murphy-Bunting, and even the 2020 draft provided immediate help in safety Antoine Winfield Jr.

Licht's relationship with Arians in Arizona helped convince the two-time NFL Coach of the Year to come out of retirement in 2019, the two envisioning a run just like this team has had.

"Jason is the main reason I came back in coaching," Arians said during the playoffs. "I knew how good of an evaluator he was … We shared the same vision. We were going to build this thing on defense. We'll score enough points … Can't say enough about what Jason has done. To me, he's Executive of the Year, just pulling off that stuff that he did."

Licht has done so without mortgaging the team's future with reckless salary-cap manipulation. The Bucs will be busy this spring, trying to retain a slew of coveted free agents, central to the team's success this season: receiver Chris Godwin, linebacker Lavonte David, Barrett, Gronkowski, defensive lineman Ndamukong Suh, Brown and Fournette, among others. Perhaps the allure of trying to go after another championship with Brady will help them take less money to return for something special.

Licht turns 50 just days after the Super Bowl, and his New England roots have taught him that sustained success, built around the right coaches and players, is very possible, but those seasons, like wins, come one at a time. As a hometown Super Bowl approached, he was above all thankful to the Glazer family, which owns the Bucs, for staying committed to whatever he needed to help build a winner in Tampa Bay.

"They wanted to be in the Super Bowl and they want to win it like we all do, but they want to do it for the fans," Licht said. "They love the excitement that the Tampa Bay fans have because of this. I think that's what drives them. I'm just very grateful." ■

Quarterback Tom Brady (12) and tight end Rob Gronkowski (87), seen here talking during training camp prior to the start of the 2020 season, picked up where they left off in New England.

Jason Licht made several key moves in constructing a Super Bowl-caliber roster, none bigger than adding the incomparable Tom Brady (12) to set the tone.

12
QUARTERBACK

TOM BRADY

Brady's Championship Pedigree Elevates Bucs to New Heights
By Greg Auman

In such a strange, unprecedented year, 2020 taught us to accept and embrace everyday phrases we'd never thought to use before, like "social distancing" and "flattening the curve" and "toilet paper shortage" and "Bucs quarterback Tom Brady."

COVID-19 and its impact on the entire sports world was the dominant storyline of the year, but you could argue an amazing second was Brady, a six-time Super Bowl champion, leaving the Patriots after 20 years and signing with the Bucs, who hadn't been to the playoffs in 13 years and hadn't won a postseason game since January 2003, back when Brady had only one ring.

The NFL had never had a 43-year-old starting quarterback for an entire season, but Brady continued to defy the normal deterioration of an athlete's skills over time. No Bucs quarterback had ever thrown for more than 33 touchdowns in a season, and he threw for 40, while helping the team commit 24 fewer turnovers than the year before.

Stats were never the true measure of Brady success, so that would come in the postseason, and the Bucs won their final four games to end their long playoff drought, but as a wild card, something Brady had never known. The Bucs had just one road playoff win in their 44-year history, but Brady helped them to three in three weeks, winning at Washington, then New Orleans, then Green Bay.

How do you make a 10th Super Bowl appearance special? You do it on your home field, which was unprecedented, and with an entirely new team, new coaches, new offense, new city, and all in the middle of a pandemic.

"As it's played out, I've just thought, 'Wow, this has really been a magical year,'" Brady said after beating the Packers to earn the right to play for a championship at home. "For me as a player to switch teams, that takes a lot. To move my family, to go to a different conference, to keep building the way we did and develop a rapport with the guys that we have here — so much of football is about the relationships that you get with your teammates, coaches. The fact that we're still playing feels really good for me and (I) understand that we've put

Tom Brady delivered exactly what the Buccaneers hoped when they signed him, helping change the culture of the team and delivering the second Super Bowl title in franchise history.

a lot into it. Hopefully we can go finish the job — that would be the best part about the season. It's always been a goal to win the last game of the year."

A year earlier, such a move seemed a real long shot — even if Brady indeed decided to leave New England, would he really choose the Bucs? Bucs coach Bruce Arians and general manager Jason Licht wanted to find out, so they took a home-run swing, and connected in every sense, signing him to a two-year, $50 million contract that immediately changed their team's identity.

Could they really envision a Super Bowl? With Brady, everything was possible.

"Naturally, I think you envision it every year in the offseason. You want to make some moves that hopefully get your team into the Super Bowl," Licht said. "I think when you sign a guy like Tom, it makes it a little more realistic. Just talking to him the days after we signed him, you could just hear and feel the confidence that he had. It made it a little bit more real. Now, you never take anything for granted. We had some highs and lows in the season where things at times looked a little grim. We needed to pull together, but we never lost our confidence. Looking back on some of the things we talked about, you do kind of want to pinch yourselves a little bit saying, 'Wow, this really did happen.' "

Once the Bucs got Brady, they lured his top Patriots target, tight end Rob Gronkowski, out of retirement and traded for his rights. They added much-needed help for the ground game in running back Leonard Fournette, and another Pro Bowl caliber receiver to go with Mike Evans and Chris Godwin in veteran Antonio Brown, who would catch five touchdowns in five games late in the year.

It wasn't always easy, of course. COVID-19 restrictions took away the entire offseason and meant no preseason games, so Brady didn't have the usual time

Coach Bruce Arians knew that he needed to improve the quarterback position after a rollercoaster 2019 season with Jameis Winston, and Tom Brady was the ideal upgrade, combining steadying, calm leadership with excellent play.

with new teammates to build chemistry and learn each other's tendencies. He threw two interceptions, one returned for a touchdown, in his Bucs debut, a loss at New Orleans. A second meeting with the Saints was a 38-3 loss, and the team dropped three of four games to fall to 7-5, barely in the playoffs as a wild card as they finally reached their bye week in Week 13.

From there, Brady and the Bucs rolled. They won their last four games, with Brady throwing 12 touchdowns and one interception (that on a deflection) to enter the postseason with momentum and confidence. Brady's Patriots success was always as a division champ, which meant home playoff games and usually a first-round bye. This time, he was a wild card, on the road for three straight wins, as many as he totaled in reaching his first nine Super Bowls combined.

Playing with Brady brought a confidence and calm to the entire locker room, including a defense that stepped up with key takeaways and stops to close out the last two playoff wins. No player has more Super Bowl experience than Brady, but in the days leading up to the big game against the Chiefs, he made it clear that past accomplishments wouldn't help him or the Bucs on Feb. 7 — that would fall on their ability to rise to the rare moment in front of them.

"Experience doesn't matter — playing well matters," he said. "The team that wins is not going to be the most experienced team, it's going to be the team that plays the best. We've got to prepare the best, we've got to execute the best, we've got to perform the best under pressure. If we do that, we'll be champions. If we don't, we won't be." ∎

Tom Brady and Bruce Arians celebrate after knocking off the Packers in Green Bay for the NFC Championship.

SAINTS 34, BUCCANEERS 23
September 13, 2020 • New Orleans, Louisiana

QUICK START, SLOW FINISH

Tom Brady's Debut with Bucs Goes Off Track in Loss to Division Rival Saints

By Joey Johnston

Tom Brady's Bucs debut did not feature blaring trumpets. Or cannon fire. Or thunderous applause. Or even a cascade of boos.

In fact, there was no noise at all.

When the National Football League season opener unfolded at the Louisiana Superdome — and the Bucs fell flat in a 34-23 defeat against the New Orleans Saints — there were no fans permitted in the cavernous 73,000-seat structure due to the COVID-19 pandemic.

"It felt like a scrimmage out there," Brady said. "But obviously, it counts."

It seemed like it counted for more than one loss because the Bucs immediately fell behind their most heated NFC South division rival. With pregame hype surrounding the historic matchup of Brady and Saints quarterback Drew Brees, the two leading passers in NFL annals, it didn't unfold as a free-flowing duel. It was more of a grind.

Brady's tenure began with a flourish, an 85-yard, nine-play scoring drive on Tampa Bay's first possession, which ended with his 2-yard sneak, punctuated by an emphatic spike.

But two Brady mistakes proved cataclysmic, opening the door wide for New Orleans.

The first of Brady's two interceptions, a miscommunication with wide receiver Mike Evans, led to Alvin Kamara's 6-yard touchdown run, which put the Saints ahead for good 14-7 in the second quarter.

Brady's second interception, nearly three minutes into the second half, was flagged by Saints cornerback Janoris Jenkins, who jumped a sideline route and returned it for a 36-yard touchdown. New Orleans led 24-7 and it suddenly looked like a runaway.

The Bucs cut it to 24-17 late in the third quarter, but ultimately couldn't overcome their mistakes. The blunders included a muffed fourth-quarter kickoff by Mike Edwards at the Tampa Bay 18-yard line, leading to a Saints' tack-on field goal. Overall, the Bucs were penalized nine times for 103 yards and had three turnovers. The Saints had none.

It was a concerning start for the Bucs, whose 7-9 season in 2019 was haunted by 41 turnovers (including 30 interceptions thrown by former quarterback Jameis Winston) and a minus-13 turnover differential, which ranked 28th in the NFL.

"There's no doubt," said Bucs coach Bruce Arians, when asked if Tampa Bay had beaten itself. "It's my job to make that stop. I thought we had it fixed. Obviously, I didn't do a very good job of getting it fixed."

Brady said he was disappointed with the mistakes.

"We have to look each other in the eye and all work harder, put more urgency on the things we have to do," Brady said. "I certainly think (it was) poor execution. That's what it comes down to. I just made some bad, terrible turnovers and it's hard to win turning over the ball like that. They were just bad throws. Can't do it."

Tom Brady and the Bucs stumbled out of the gate against the division rival Saints, a fortuitous parallel with the 2002 Super Bowl champion Tampa Bay squad.

Brady finished 23 of 36 for 239 yards and two touchdowns, one to tight end O.J. Howard and the other to Evans (with 2:41 remaining for his only catch of the game). The Saints managed just 271 total yards — and only 160 passing from Brees.

But the Saints didn't need anything more. Tampa Bay's mistakes made sure of that.

"He (Brady) knows how to bounce back," Arians said. "He knew he didn't play very well and it's not what he expects from himself. I would anticipate him to have a little more grit (and) a little more determination (heading into practice).

"I think it's a great learning experience. It's just Round 1 of a 16-round fight and we'll learn from it."

Even in the grisly aftermath, optimistic Bucs fans pointed out that the greatest season in franchise history (2002) also began 0-1.

Déjà vu: Jon Gruden's Bucs opened with a loss against the Saints.

Ultimately, those Bucs captured the Super Bowl XXXVII championship.

It became a coincidence well worth filing away. ∎

BUCCANEERS 31, PANTHERS 17
September 20, 2020 • Tampa, Florida

ON THE BOARD

Bucs Pull Away Late in First Win of the Season

By Joey Johnston

Bucs coach Bruce Arians said it best: "Turnovers come in bunches."

One week after getting no takeaways, the Bucs became big-time opportunists in a 31-17 victory against the Carolina Panthers at Raymond James Stadium.

The Bucs (1-1) collected an interception and a fumble recovery during a three-play offensive span for the Panthers (0-2), leading to a pair of Tampa Bay first-quarter touchdowns and a 21-0 halftime advantage.

But even with four total takeaways, the Bucs were on the verge of a giveaway.

The Panthers hung around, chipping away, watching the Bucs slumber, then pulling within 24-17 on Joey Slye's 23-yard field goal with 1:57 remaining. Slye then tried an onside kick, but it was recovered by Tampa Bay's Rob Gronkowski at the Carolina 46-yard line.

That seemed like the punctuation mark.

But there was a final exclamation point.

On the first play, Leonard Fournette, the former two-time 1,000-yard rusher with the Jacksonville Jaguars who had been a Buc for less than two weeks, rumbled for a 46-yard score to give him 103 yards on his 12-carry day.

"I tried to put the icing on the cake for the team," Fournette said.

Overall, though, this game was anything but a piece of cake.

Through the offseason — a combination of giddiness (the signing of Brady) and bizarre inactivity (the pandemic) — the Bucs had been painted as an organization that was not only ready for the next step, it was probably the NFC's Super Bowl favorite. Could 16-0 be far behind?

Bucs coach Bruce Arians provided all the requisite reality checks in his training-camp remarks, but the true warning shot came in a season-opening 34-23 loss at New Orleans. The home opener wasn't a must-win situation, but high-expectation fans couldn't stomach 0-2.

Was this one perfect? Hardly.

Was it uneven? Definitely.

But it was a start, some movement in the right direction.

Quarterback Tom Brady was 23 of 35 for 217 yards and a touchdown. Wide receiver Mike Evans, after a one-catch opener, answered with seven receptions for 104 yards and a 23-yard score. And there was also Fournette, whose long touchdown gave him an average of 8.6 yards per rush.

"Our execution was a little bit better," Brady said. "I think we are still a long ways from where we need to be.

Wide receiver Mike Evans had a big day against the Panthers, catching seven passes for 104 yards and a touchdown.

Consistency and dependability are going to be things that we really need. We've got to get back to work. The clock is ticking."

Brady also bounced back in Week 2 after dropping openers with the New England Patriots in 2003, 2014 and 2017.

"He has a pretty good history of that," Arians said. "This game should have never gotten to as close as it did. But I thought he was outstanding. His leadership on the sideline was great, and he put us in the right play with a number of different audibles and played really, really well."

Brady, though, quickly shifted credit to another unit.

"Our defense played great the first two games and we've got to match them," Brady said.

An interception by safety Jordan Whitehead set up a 10-play, 78-yard touchdown drive — fueled by Brady's 50-yard pass to Evans — with running back Ronald Jones scoring from the 7. On Carolina's possession, rookie safety Antoine Winfield Jr. registered a second-down sack of Panthers quarterback Teddy Bridgewater, who lost a fumble to Jason Pierre-Paul. On the next play, Brady hit Evans on a 23-yard touchdown.

The Bucs were rolling.

Or so it seemed.

Ultimately, there were lessons to be learned. The Panthers still gained 427 yards, so the four takeaways and five sacks of Bridgewater helped preserve the winning margin. But it was more fun to learn from a victory.

"We're 1-1," Arians said. "It's 16 games. Like I just told the guys, 'Are we going to show up any different this week because we won versus last week when we lost? No.' We're going to come to work and get ready for the next one."

"I've always been coached to not get too high and not get too low," Evans said. "Hopefully all the guys have that mindset where this is just one win. We just got beat down last week. We can't forget that. We definitely want to string these wins together and do what we are capable of doing. And that's being a great team."

Fournette, who also scored on a 1-yard second-quarter run, showed that the Bucs have one of the key dimensions for a great team — depth.

"It's nice to have a hell of a player with fresh legs in the fourth quarter," Arians said. "We did a good job, I thought, of mixing the backs in. As Leonard keeps practicing, learning and doing some things, we'll keep getting him more and more touches."

"You are so used to being the guy," Fournette said. "But you get your breath back with the rotation of the backs, so it's helping. It's a team sport at the end of the day. Don't just think about yourself. There is a bigger picture than yourself." ∎

Defensive end Jason Pierre-Paul (90) and linebacker Devin White (45) combine to take down Carolina Panthers running back Christian McCaffrey (22) during the second half of the Tampa Bay win.

BUCCANEERS 28, BRONCOS 10
September 27, 2020 • Denver, Colorado

A DEFENSIVE TRADITION

Tampa Bay Rides Tough Defense, Cruises to Second Victory

By Joey Johnston

Understandably, Tom Brady's presence fueled grand ambitions for the Bucs. The arrival of other luminaries, such as Rob Gronkowski and Leonard Fournette, increased that optimism. Holdovers such as Mike Evans and Chris Godwin made the imagination race.

But the Bucs' franchise heritage was built around defense. To again reach the championship level, defense must be at the forefront.

"There's no doubt, we built this team on defense," Bucs coach Bruce Arians said. "Tom (Brady) was just the icing on the cake. When we came into the offseason last year, (we said) 'Hey, let's keep this defense together because it can be special.' "

It was extra special in a 28-10 road victory against the Denver Broncos (0-3).

With defensive coordinator Todd Bowles dialing up an array of blitzes — involving the linemen, linebackers and secondary — the Bucs (2-1) collected six sacks and 10 hits on Bronco quarterbacks.

"That's what we try to do, don't do the same thing over and over, just throw different things at them," Bucs linebacker Lavonte David said. "And the good thing about it is once you understand what your job is and understand what the job is of guys around you, it gives you the opportunity to play faster.

"And it gives you the opportunity to disguise and show different looks to the quarterback. That's what we try to do, man, and once we get a team one-dimensional, coach always says he's going to unload it. Once you've got everybody in the playbook understanding what Coach Bowles wants? Oh man, we can be the best."

Linebacker Shaquil Barrett, who led the NFL in sacks (19 1/2) during 2019, had his first two sacks of the season and one was when he trapped Broncos quarterback Jeff Driskel in the end zone for a safety. Sacks were also registered by defensive tackle Vita Vea and linebacker Jason Pierre-Paul, along with safeties Antoine Winfield Jr. and Jordan Whitehead.

For good measure, Mike Edwards had an end-zone interception and defensive lineman Patrick O'Connor blocked a punt on the Broncos' first series, leading to the Bucs' first score, a 10-yard pass from Brady to Godwin.

Overall, the Broncos were limited to 226 total yards. Four possessions went three-and-out. Only a late fourth-quarter drive allowed the Broncos to surpass the 200-yard mark.

"Coach Bowles knows what he's doing," Barrett said. "He's most definitely a defensive guru. We appreciate him always getting us on the right page and telling us what needs to be fixed. He has a great defensive mind."

Bowles, though, put the credit on his players.

Safety Jordan Whitehead (33) and the Bucs' defense made it hard on quarterback Brett Rypien (4) and the Broncos throughout the game, holding Denver to only 10 points.

"I think it's just their second year in the system and them trusting each other on the field," Bowles said. "I think as coaches, it's our job to try to put them in the best positions possible for them to make a play. Believe me, we're no masterminds over here at all. We just try to coach good football and good football players. We work hard every week.

"Sometimes, you have a good game plan and it (stinks). Sometimes, you have a bad game plan and it works out well. We're just going to keep grinding and working."

Bowles said he realizes the Bucs' array of offensive weapons — along with Brady's efficient management — gives his defense plenty of chances to thrive as well.

Once again, Tampa Bay's offense took another step forward. For the first time in almost a decade (Nov. 14-21, 2010), the Bucs won back-to-back games by 14 or more points.

Brady was 25 of 38 for 297 yards with three touchdowns and no interceptions. Two of his TDs were 1-yarders to Evans on consecutive second-quarter possessions, giving the Bucs a 23-3 advantage.

Brady utilized eight different receivers, each with at least two catches.

"I think everybody contributed," Brady said. "Ultimately, everyone who is dressed is going to have to be ready to go. We've got to keep turning it up a notch.

"We're getting there. It's a long process. This (today's game) would have been our third preseason game. There's a lot to learn, a lot of room to grow. We're getting to know each other, accomplishing things and making things happen."

Evans, the Bucs' top receiver, was a big part of that.

"He's a great red-area threat with his size, his quickness, his elusiveness, his hands, everything," Brady said. "Mike is one of the great receivers in the NFL. I've got to find ways to get him the ball, get it to him in space, not just in the red-area, but all over the field."

But the Bucs receiver with the most catches against the Broncos was Gronkowski, Brady's former teammate with the New England Patriots who was coaxed out of retirement to join Tampa Bay. Through two games, he had mostly been invisible — "I came here to block, baby!" he playfully chided — but emerged with six receptions for 48 yards against the Broncos.

"It just felt good to be out there and making a couple of plays," Gronkowski said. "You won't get targets your way every week because you never know how the game's going to go. But today, it went that way, where I had a lot of targets. The way Tom spreads the ball out is unbelievable. He always finds the open guy."

Gronkowski said he has heard "garbage" about Brady since first joining him 10 years ago, constant talk that "he didn't have anything left in the tank."

"That's simply not true," Gronkowski said. "Just the way he can air the ball out and put a dime where he needs to … overall as an offense I feel like we can come together better, start feeling each other out and make even more plays." ∎

Mike Evans only had two catches in the win, but both went for touchdowns, two of the 13 he caught during the season.

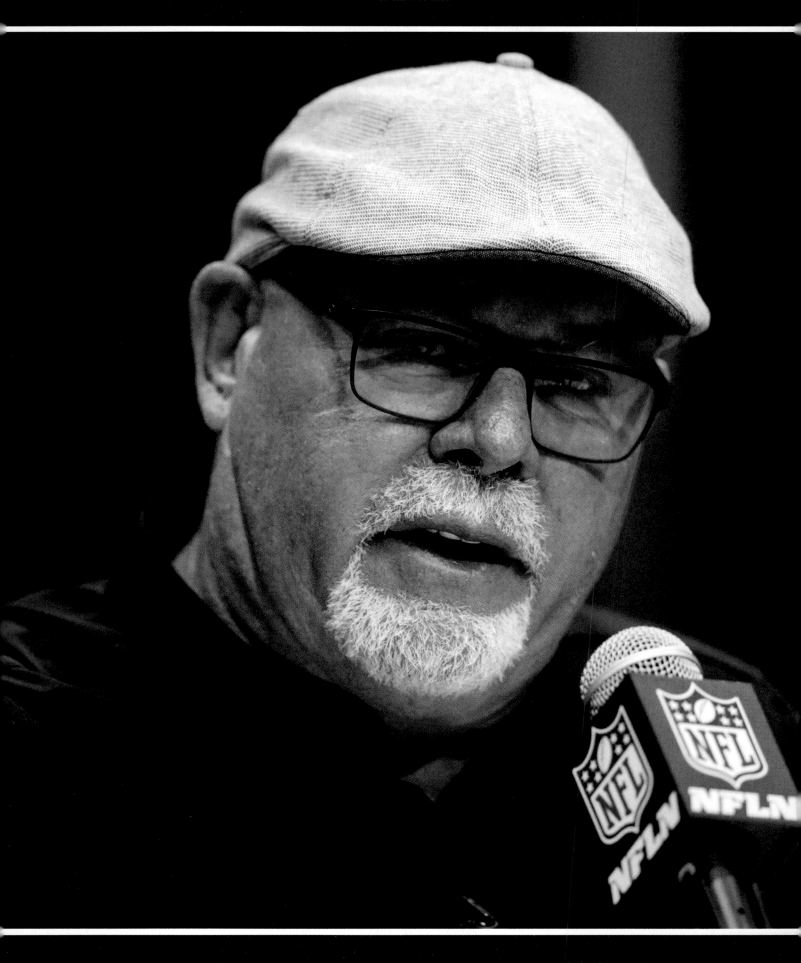

HEAD COACH

BRUCE ARIANS

Arians Leads Bucs Through Unprecedented Season to Unforgettable Results

By Greg Auman

Bruce Arians had won two Super Bowls as an assistant, had twice been named NFL Coach of the Year, but the improbability of 2020, the way his Bucs team came together in the middle of a pandemic, it made this something special.

"This has been the most rewarding year of coaching in my life," he said moments after the Bucs pulled out a 31-26 win over the Packers to become the first NFL team ever to earn the right to play a Super Bowl on their home field.

It was rewarding because it was difficult, in every way. Arians, 68, had come out of retirement a year earlier, finishing a disappointing 7-9 in his first season in Tampa. The surprising addition of Tom Brady created an excitement, but it would be four months before Arians got to work with him in person, after a long summer in isolation, unsure of when or if the season would be played.

Wouldn't it be the Bucs' luck that they sign Brady, trade for Rob Gronkowski and all but sell out their stadium to excited, win-starved fans, only to have a season cancelled by COVID-19? But the season pushed on as scheduled, Tampa Bay burdened with the unfair expectations that come with a six-time Super Bowl champion joining a franchise that hadn't made the playoffs in 13 years.

"I was amused when they handed us the Lombardi trophy in July. It's part of the business," Arians said after a season-opening loss at the Saints. "You go with it and it's one week at a time [and] one day at a time. We win a few games in a row and everybody will be back on the bandwagon, happy. It's just part of the game. If we lose this week, the world will come to an end."

The Bucs didn't lose that week, and halfway through the season, they were 6-2, affirming all those high preseason hopes. Tampa Bay had no offseason and no

Bruce Arians and the Bucs wasted no time responding to a disappointing 7-9 season in 2019, making one of the biggest free agency splashes in NFL history by signing Tom Brady.

preseason games to build a much-needed chemistry with
so many new parts, so the offense was still a work in
progress, the defense still inconsistent from week to week.

That caught up to the Bucs as they took a one-point
loss at the Bears, and later a pair of three-point losses
to the Rams and Chiefs, leaving them at 7-5 and unsure
if they'd make the playoffs at all. Tampa Bay had a late
bye in Week 13 and came back refreshed and refocused,
bouncing back with a home win against the Vikings.

On both sides of the ball, the Bucs still had issues
with slow starts, at one point being outscored 59-7 in
the first quarter over a six-game span. In Week 15, that
meant Tampa Bay was down 17-0 at the half at the lowly
Falcons, humbled and outgained 261-60. But the Bucs
woke up in a big way after halftime, scoring touchdowns
on three straight drives. They tied the game in the fourth
quarter, then won it on a 46-yard touchdown pass from
Brady to receiver Antonio Brown.

Brown was a controversial signing at midseason,
giving Brady another top-tier receiver to go with
Mike Evans and Chris Godwin but risking the club's
chemistry. He had no touchdowns in his first five games
with Tampa Bay, but the late score against Atlanta set
off a run of five touchdowns in five games, sparking an
improved offense as the Bucs ended the regular season
on a four-game win streak.

What Arians did in the postseason was even
more impressive, facing a tougher path as a wild card,
something Brady had never done in 20 years in New
England. The Bucs won a close game at Washington,
then forced four turnovers in a revenge win at New
Orleans, which had swept them in the regular season.

Seeking a third straight road win, they went to
snowy Green Bay — where the Bucs were 1-15 over a

Head coach Bruce Arians proved to be the perfect
leader to navigate the Bucs through an NFL season
unlike any other on the way to winning his first Super
Bowl as the man in charge.

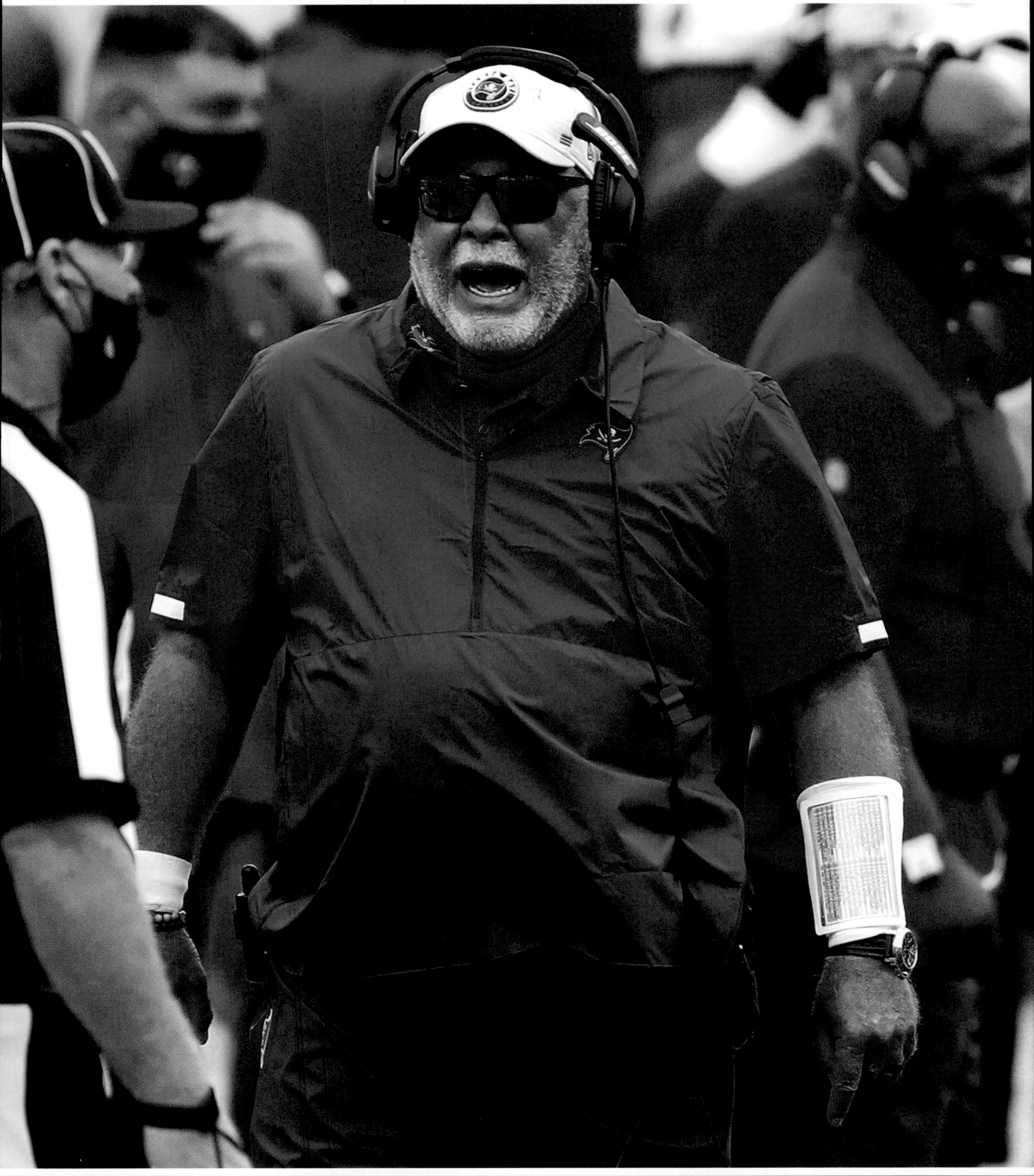

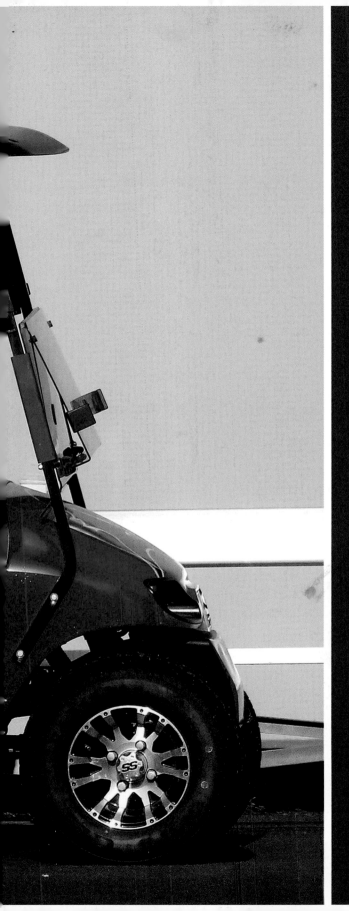

30-year span — and Arians was at his boldest and best. With 13 seconds left in the first half and clinging to a four-point lead, he called his punt team off the field, went for it on fourth down, got the conversion and then stunned the Packers as Brady threw a 39-yard touchdown to receiver Scotty Miller with one second left in the half. The Packers wouldn't go away, and Brady uncharacteristically threw interceptions on three straight possessions in the second half, but his defense stepped up and closed out a huge, franchise-changing win.

All year long, the question was what would constitute success for the Bucs — they hadn't made the playoffs since 2007, so doing so would be a major step forward, but a small accomplishment by Brady's postseason standards. But making a Super Bowl for only the second time in franchise history, and doing so on their home field, was inarguably an enormous source of pride for all involved, especially the head coach.

Holding the George Halas Trophy as NFC champions in the cold of Lambeau Field, Arians was quick to thank his assistants and players for such a memorable win, and in closing, was asked his message to the fans back in Tampa.

"We're coming home, and we're coming home to win!" he said. ∎

Bruce Arians successfully juggled the high preseason expectations for the Bucs, as well as a locker room full of established veterans and colorful personalities.

BUCCANEERS 38, CHARGERS 31
October 4, 2020 • Tampa, Florida

WHAT A DIFFERENCE A BRADY MAKES

Tom Brady and Bucs Prevail in Shootout Over Chargers

By Joey Johnston

What a difference a Brady makes.

When the Bucs rallied from a 17-point second-quarter deficit to stun the Los Angeles Chargers 38-31 at Raymond James Stadium, it was clear that the franchise had made a quantum leap.

Not only in personnel, but in mindset.

"I can honestly say had this been last year, we'd have gotten our (butts) beat by 20 (points)," Bucs coach Bruce Arians said. "This team has a ton of character and playmakers. We started making plays and you can see when we don't beat ourselves, we're going to be a tough team to beat."

And with Tom Brady at quarterback, the Bucs believe they can win any game.

"How can you not believe in him?" Bucs wide receiver Scotty Miller said. "He's the greatest to ever do it."

Brady completed 30 of 46 passes for 369 yards and tied a club record with five touchdown tosses (to five different players). Trailing 24-7, the Bucs (3-1) scored three unanswered touchdowns. When the Chargers (1-3) regained their lead heading into the fourth quarter, Brady engineered a seven-play, 75-yard drive that gave Tampa Bay the advantage for good.

"Tom is never behind in his mind," Arians said.

That's how it looked, even in the dismal early going when Brady threw a pick-six — a 78-yard interception return by defensive back Michael Davis — and the Chargers rallied around rookie quarterback Justin Herbert.

For an NFL-record 34th time, Brady overcame a deficit or 10 or more points to win (including the postseason). It was the 46th time Brady led a winning drive in the fourth quarter or overtime of a regular-season game, which ranks fourth all-time behind Peyton Manning (54), Drew Brees (50) and Dan Marino (47).

"We put ourselves in a pretty good hole and we were going to have to dig our way out of it," Brady said. "That's just the way football works sometimes. We started the game well and finished the game well. That middle part? We have to figure out how to play 60 minutes well.

"And the defense made a big play for us before the end of the (first) half. That got us ignited a little bit."

The defense made a huge play indeed.

Tom Brady had a huge game against the Chargers, completing 30 of 46 passes for 369 yards and five touchdowns.

The Bucs were ready to slink into halftime and repair their wounds. The Chargers, leading 24-7, were at their 9-yard line with 38 seconds remaining. Instead of taking a knee, the Chargers took an unnecessary chance. Herbert handed to running back Joshua Kelley, who was stripped by Bucs defensive tackle Ndamukong Suh and linebacker Devin White recovered at the 6. Three plays later, Brady found wide receiver Mike Evans for a 6-yard touchdown and the Bucs had closed to within 24-14.

Momentum had changed.

"I jumped the gap and saw an opportunity to make a play," Suh said. "It created some momentum for us. Tom and offense did a great job punching it in. That's what we have to do as a defense — make sure we give them as many opportunities to score points because we know we have plenty of firepower over there."

"I was a bit surprised they didn't just take a knee," Evans said. "It was 24-7. They'd had a great first half. They made a mistake. We capitalized on it, got a touchdown and had momentum going into the second half and ran with it."

And passed with it, too.

After the Chargers went three-and-out to begin the third quarter, Brady went 5-for-5 on a 69-yard drive, finishing with a 28-yard scoring pass to tight end O.J. Howard, making it 24-21.

Suddenly, the Chargers could do nothing right. Michael Badgley was wide left on a 44-yard field-goal attempt, and Brady wasted no time. He hit Miller with a 44-yard pass, then a 19-yard score and the Bucs led 28-24.

The Chargers still wouldn't go away.

On the third quarter's final play, Herbert found Jalen Guyton on a riveting 73-yard catch-and-run touchdown. The Bucs were trailing again, 31-28, but only briefly. It was rookie running back Ke'Shawn Vaughn on the receiving end of a 9-yard score to complete a seven-play, 75-yard drive and the Bucs led 35-31.

From there, it was Ryan Succop's 26-yard insurance field goal and cornerback Carlton Davis sealing it with an interception of Herbert at the Bucs' 48-yard line with 2:22 remaining.

"We just had to get our heads out of our butts, make some plays and be aggressive," Davis said of the defensive halftime adjustments. "Any given Sunday, all kind of obstacles are going to occur and it's all about how you battle back."

There was the improved Bucs' defense. And, of course, there was Brady, who used diverse weapons, including Evans (seven catches for 122 yards), running back Ronald Jones (who rushed 20 times for 111 yards, making for an effective play-action approach), Miller (five catches for 83 yards) and Howard (three catches for 50 yards, although he suffered a season-ending Achilles injury).

"He's the G.O.A.T. (Greatest Of All Time), that's as simple as I can put it," Davis said. "Having him go down and score touchdowns gives us a lot more energy and just gives the whole sideline more confidence."

What a difference a Brady makes. ∎

Tight end Cameron Brate (84) was one of five different Buccaneers with a receiving touchdown, his lone catch of the day for a 3-yard score.

BEARS 20, BUCCANEERS 19

October 8, 2020 • Chicago, Illinois

CONFUSION REIGNS

Rally Falls Short on Final Drive in Ugly Loss to Bears

By Joey Johnston

The Bucs had not played well on a short week — not by anyone's estimation — but they seemed on the verge of pulling out an ugly Thursday night road victory against the Chicago Bears at Soldier Field.

It was fourth-and-6 at the Tampa Bay 41-yard line. The chains had to be moved — maybe twice — for a realistic winning field-goal attempt.

Quarterback Tom Brady threw down the seam for tight end Cameron Brate, but the pass was knocked away by Chicago's DeAndre Houston-Carson. Thirty-three seconds remained. That was that.

Bears 20, Bucs 19.

Game over.

But when television cameras focused on Brady, he wore a confused look and held up four fingers, as if he thought there was another play remaining.

Confusion reigned in the postgame, when Bucs coach Bruce Arians insisted that Brady had not lost track of the downs.

"He knew (it was fourth down)," Arians said.

Brady was twice asked about the final play, but his answers were evasive.

"Yeah, I knew we needed a chunk and I was thinking about more yardage," Brady said. "It was just bad execution. We had a great opportunity there. Just didn't execute when we needed to.

"Yeah, you're up against the clock and you're up against the … I knew we had to gain a chunk, so I

should have been thinking more first down instead of chunk in that situation."

The question was never fully answered. One day later, Arians said, "I don't know how to answer it for him. We all knew it was fourth down. I think he saw what he saw."

The Brady/four fingers photo became an Internet sensation. Brady, a Twitter/Instagram jokester, photoshopped LeBron James' head on the Brady body with the four fingers extended and wrote: "Congrats to my brother @KingJames on winning his 4th championship. Not bad for a washed up old guy!"

The bottom line?

The Bucs (3-2) had to settle for four field goals by Ryan Succop (three from 39 yards and in). They had 11 penalties for 109 yards and were only 4-for-14 on third-down conversions.

The Bucs put themselves in position to lose. They blew a 13-point lead in the second quarter and never recovered.

Call it a four-gone conclusion.

"We were shooting ourselves in the foot," said Bucs running back Ronald Jones, a bright spot with 106 yards rushing. "No way we should've lost that game."

The Bucs found that way.

"I think turnovers, penalties, field position all those lead to points," said Brady, summing up a night that also saw the loss of defensive tackle Vita Vea to a fractured ankle. "It comes down to third down, red-area, ultimately, you are trying to score more points than the other team.

After the Bears' defense knocked away Tom Brady's fourth-down pass late in the fourth quarter, the Buccaneers' quarterback wore a confused look and held up for fingers, as if he thought there was another play remaining.

Turnovers are a big part of it and penalties are another big part of that because you are not possessing the football if you are third and long yardage. You need to have clean games where you stay ahead on down and distance."

Succop sandwiched two made field goals around Brady's 2-yard touchdown pass to Mike Evans and the Bucs led 13-0 midway through the second quarter. It looked oh so routine.

But the Bears (4-1) rallied around Nick Foles, the former Super Bowl Most Valuable Player (with the Eagles) who made his second start in Chicago. Foles was 30 of 42 passing for 243 yards.

The game turned in a flash when the Bears scored two touchdowns in the final 1:48 of the half. David Montgomery got Chicago on the board with a 3-yard run.

On the ensuing possession, Bucs running back Ke'Shawn Vaughn fumbled after a big hit from Kyle Fuller and Robert Quinn recovered at the Bucs' 27-yard line. Four plays later, Foles found Jimmy Graham for a 12-yard score, a one-handed grab despite the tight defense of cornerback Jamel Dean that gave Chicago a 14-13 halftime advantage.

The second half was a procession of field goals, two for each team. Succop's 25-yarder put the Bucs up 19-17 with 4:49 to play. But the Bears answered back and got a 38-yarder from Cairo Santos with 1:13 remaining.

That set up the finish.

And the four-gone conclusion. ∎

BUCCANEERS 38, PACKERS 10

October 18, 2020 • Tampa, Florida

FOOT ON THE GAS

Buccaneers Overcome Early Deficit, Steamroll Shocked Packers

By Joey Johnston

It was the game when things started coming together for the Bucs. And it was typified by the atypical facial expressions from Green Bay Packers quarterback Aaron Rodgers, the ultimate cool customer.

This was disbelief.

This was shock.

The previously unbeaten Packers were steamrolled by the Bucs 38-10 at wind-swept Raymond James Stadium. By the second half, there was no suspense. Green Bay's final seven possessions ended with a punt.

Early on, it looked like a runaway — for the Packers (4-1), who raced to a 10-point lead. Then everything changed early in the second quarter.

Rodgers' third-and-10 pass was intercepted by Bucs cornerback Jamel Dean and returned for a 32-yard touchdown.

Packers 10, Bucs 7.

Three plays later, Rodgers was intercepted again, this time by Mike Edwards, who nearly took it to the end zone before being tripped up at the 2-yard line. Ronald Jones scored from there.

Bucs 14, Packers 10.

And it was over.

Some perspective: To that point, Rodgers had played in 193 NFL games. He had surrendered just two pick-six interceptions. Then, in the space of four pass attempts, he nearly delivered two more. Disbelief? Shock? The turnaround was stunning and the Bucs (4-2) were roaring.

"Dean made his play and that kind of changed the whole momentum — I thought — in the whole stadium," Bucs coach Bruce Arians said. "That pick-six changed the whole ballgame."

Beyond that, though, the Bucs played a textbook game.

No penalties.

No turnovers.

No sacks allowed.

Meanwhile, Tampa Bay's defense had five sacks of Rodgers and 13 quarterback hits (Rodgers had been sacked just three times in four previous games).

"You know we have great stars on the offensive side of the ball, but we want this team to be a defensive team," Bucs linebacker Devin White said. "We want to be the guys on the field when it's crunch time. We want to be the ones to make that play or get us off the field and get our offense the ball back. I think we showed just that."

Tampa Bay's offense had nice moments, too.

Quarterback Tom Brady was efficient, going 17 for 27 with 166 yards and two touchdowns, one to veteran tight end Rob Gronkowski (five catches, 78 yards) and the other to rookie wide receiver Tyler Johnson. Jones had 23 carries for 113 yards and two touchdowns as he

Linebacker Devin White sacks Green Bay quarterback Aaron Rodgers, one of five sacks on the day for the Tampa Bay defense.

registered his third consecutive 100-yard rushing performance.

"We just had to keep our foot on the gas," Jones said. "We started off a little slow, then the defense picked us up and we kept the momentum and kept riding with it. We didn't let up."

The defense got it started and the offense finished things off. It was a 28-point second quarter for the Bucs. There was an entire half to play, but the Packers were essentially done. They never got under way again. It seemed like child's play for Bucs defensive coordinator Todd Bowles, who mixed the looks, coverages and blitzes.

"You don't usually get Aaron confused," Arians said. "I don't think I've ever seen him confused. Early in the game, he made a lot of plays. We just kept chasing. It hemmed him up a little bit and we got some hits on him. The defensive line, linebackers and the secondary — it was a great defensive performance."

A seminal moment occurred after the Packers had gone up 10-0, when Bowles gathered his defensive players on the bench.

"Todd Bowles just told us, 'We're respecting these guys too much,' " White said. "He said 'They've got to earn our respect and play them honest. Just be ballhawks and get after them.' And I think once he said that, he kind of gave everyone the green light to go make plays.

"I'd say Dean's pick set the tempo for the rest of the game. We knew those guys didn't deserve to be on the field with us because we've got too much talent and fly around to the ball. And the thing is, we always have fun."

Dean said he felt good about things when he recognized the formation, checked Packers wide receiver Davante Adams and gathered in the game-turning interception.

"When I saw the formation and I saw how everything started to develop, I was like, 'I have to make this play because I know what's coming,' " Dean said. "And once I saw him throw it, I was like, 'Yeah, it's mine.' "

Once the Bucs put up their second-quarter flurry, the second half was spent playing keep away. It was a fun stance — and the Packers were largely helpless.

"I thought the offensive line played outstanding," Arians said. "Just to take that game over in the fourth quarter running the football like that — that's a joy to see."

That was how it looked for the Bucs — joy, happiness, fun.

But for Rodgers, after a good start, it was shock and disbelief. ∎

Bucs' cornerback Jamel Dean (35) heads to the end zone after intercepting Aaron Rodgers in the second quarter of the dominating win over the Packers.

BUCCANEERS 45, RAIDERS 20

October 25, 2020 • Las Vegas, Nevada

CHILD'S PLAY

Bucs Blast Gruden and Raiders on the Way to Fifth Win

By Joey Johnston

For longtime fans of the Bucs, this was a familiar sight: The sneer, the arched eyebrow, the intensity, the Chucky face. Sure enough, it was Jon Gruden, architect of Tampa Bay's first Super Bowl championship. Now with the Las Vegas Raiders — and unpleasantly on the business end of a 45-20 spanking by the Bucs at Allegiant Stadium — Gruden didn't exactly roll the dice with his postgame analysis.

"Tampa Bay was an impressive football team," Gruden said. "They have an arsenal of weapons."

Uh-huh.

Quarterback Tom Brady wasn't sacked. The Raiders (3-3) hit him only once all afternoon. So the results were predictable.

Brady was 33 of 45 for 369 yards with four touchdowns and no interceptions, giving him a quarterback rating of 127.0.

There was tight end Rob Gronkowski rumbling into the end zone with a 5-yard touchdown. There was hiccup-quick wide receiver Scotty Miller getting behind the defense for a 33-yard score just before halftime. There was reliable pass-catcher Chris Godwin making it a two-score game in the fourth quarter with a 4-yard touchdown. There was rookie receiver Tyler Johnson on a 1-yard score for the final margin.

And that doesn't even account for Mike Evans, the best of them all, who had a quiet two-catch effort.

An arsenal, indeed.

But afterward, even as the Bucs (5-2) reveled in their immensely satisfying victory, everyone wanted to talk about the real news of the day, perhaps a gamble, but definitely an indication that Tampa Bay was putting all of its chips on the table.

The Bucs were on the verge of signing Pro Bowl receiver Antonio Brown, ultra-talented but occasionally troubled and star-crossed. Big-time help was on the way for Brady's bunch … even though there were no indications the Bucs actually needed such assistance.

"It's an insurance policy," Bucs coach Bruce Arians said. "When we don't have Mike (Evans) and we don't have Chris (Godwin), why not have another Pro Bowl-caliber player that's available, that fits our camp and fits everything else? So why not? We have good players. You can't have enough of them. Why not have another one?

"Everybody wants to say that Tom (Brady) picked him. Tom didn't have nothing to do with it. This was something Jason (Licht, general manager) and I have been talking about for a couple weeks, ever since the injuries to our other (receivers). When the time was right, would we see if we could pull the trigger and fit

Rookie safety Antoine Winfield Jr. (31) picked up the first interception of his career in the commanding win over the Raiders.

it into what we want to get done. We'll see. If Antonio does what I think he's going to do, he'll be fine."

Brady, who was a believer during Brown's brief tenure with the New England Patriots in 2019, was enthused by the possibilities.

"He's a tremendous football player," Brady said. "He's a very hard-working guy. We're going to all go on the practice field and do what we can do and see how it all fits together."

Without Brown, it fit together perfectly against the Raiders.

Arians was particularly pleased with the play of Godwin (nine catches for 88 yards) and Miller (six catches for 109 yards, including the 33-yard score that made it 21-10 at halftime). Miller said he benefited from the Raiders paying extra attention to Evans.

"Mike is one of the most unselfish superstars in the league," Miller said. "He only had a couple catches today and the past couple games, but that's because he's getting double-teamed the whole game, really. That makes it so much easier for me and everybody else."

"I thought the drive at the end of the half was big in the ballgame," Arians said. "I thought it flipped the whole game around to get a touchdown before the half and finish it. We knew the way they were going to play Mike (Evans), that Scotty was going to have a game and have opportunities."

As for Godwin, the Bucs' No. 2 option at receiver continued to ascend in Arians' eyes.

"He's right there with some guys that I've had like Reggie Wayne, Larry Fitzgerald, Hines Ward," Arians said. "He can do the receiver dirty work and go down the field. That's the thing he has over all of them.

"He's a deep threat when he's healthy, and to me, he is the ultimate football player. He blocks like a tight end. He runs routes like the best receiver in

the league, inside or outside, and that's why he is so valuable to our offense."

For all the Bucs' firepower, the Raiders made a game of it. Daniel Carlson's 36-yard field goal with 12:43 remaining cut Tampa Bay's lead to 24-20. Gruden said he considered going for it on fourth-and-1 from Tampa Bay's 17-yard line but chose the safer route and relied on his defense.

Brady, though, suffocated any Raider hopes with a 21-point blitz on three consecutive possessions.

Facing third-and-13 from the Bucs' 30, Brady checked down to running back Leonard Fournette, who got exactly the needed yardage. That sparked an 11-play, 67-yard drive and Godwin's touchdown to make it 31-20.

On the ensuing possession, Raiders quarterback Derek Carr was intercepted by rookie safety Antoine Winfield Jr. — after a tip by Mike Edwards — and he returned it 16 yards to the Raider 24. Brady hit Godwin for 23, then running back Ronald Jones bulled in from the 1.

"It was a great feeling to get my first (NFL) interception," Winfield said. "Mike (Edwards) was able to defend the ball and it just came straight to me. It actually felt amazing."

The whole afternoon was amazing. A 25-point road victory. Brady's five-game run (15 touchdown passes, one interception). Everything clicking. Antonio Brown on the way. Leaving Las Vegas, the Bucs had reached what seemed like the season's highest peak. ■

Wide receiver Tyler Johnson (18) had two catches on the day, including this 1-yard touchdown in the fourth quarter.

54
LINEBACKER

LAVONTE DAVID

After Spending Entire Career with Bucs, David Relishes Breakthrough Season for Franchise

By Greg Auman

Long before Tom Brady or even Bruce Arians came to town, fans looking for signs of greatness to come in the 2020 season saw something special when Super Bowl LV was awarded to Tampa, the Roman numerals translating to 55, a number proudly retired by the Bucs in honor of Pro Football Hall of Fame linebacker Derrick Brooks.

Brooks, who spent his entire 14-year career with the Bucs, was a prominent part of the game as co-chair of the Super Bowl Host Committee, but the two letters also point to another respected veteran linebacker at the heart of a Bucs Super Bowl run: LVD, fan shorthand for Lavonte David.

Brooks was in his eighth season in 2002 when he guided a dominant Bucs defense to the Super Bowl, and David was in his ninth season in 2020, doing the same as a leader and playmaker while perpetually underappreciated for the NFL's highest honors.

"Lavonte is solid every week. He makes us go,"

defensive coordinator Todd Bowles said in October. "He's our leader. He's our emotional leader, he's our field leader, he's our general. He just makes plays all over the field, but he plays the right way. He understands run blocking, he understands pass concepts, he understands where he needs to be on the field, he understands angles. He's just a good football player."

All season, every week, it was David who walked to midfield before the game for the coin toss, the unquestioned captain. Like Brooks, he wasn't a vocal rah-rah type, rather a lead-by-example player, his contributions on the field doing the talking.

And when the Bucs clinched their first playoff berth in 13 years with a commanding 47-7 win at Detroit in Week 16, the day after Christmas, no one could appreciate how much that meant more than David, the team's longest-tenured (and thus longest-suffering) player.

"It's amazing," David said after the Detroit win.

Lavonte David and the Bucs finally broke through in his ninth season with the team, going from perennially missing the playoffs to winning a championship.

"It's a great feeling, and everybody knows what it took. Nothing's going to be given. You've got to go out and take what you want. And we did it, man. We clinched a playoff berth. That's not it, but I'm going to enjoy this moment, for sure."

David had been there from the start of the 2020 season, coming out of the gates strong enough to be NFC Defensive Player of the Month for September. He had forced and recovered a fumble in the Bucs' first win of the season against Carolina and had an interception in an early win at Denver. He had 1.5 sacks in the regular season win over Green Bay, three tackles for loss against the Rams and forced fumbles late in the year against the Lions and Falcons.

When the Bucs needed one last stop to seal their first playoff victory in nearly 18 years, it was David who blitzed and sacked Washington quarterback Taylor Heinicke on third down, setting up a desperation fourth-and-long heave that fell incomplete.

David's statistical dominance is nearly unmatched among NFL inside linebackers, and yet in nine seasons, he has only one Pro Bowl selection and one first-team All-Pro nod to show for it. Those perennial snubs will be the biggest thing working against him having a résumé good enough to follow Brooks to Canton and a spot in the Pro Football Hall of Fame, but helping a team to the Super Bowl is another valuable criteria that now works in his favor.

An inside linebacker's most prolific stat will always be tackles, and with other retirements this season, David now ranks as the NFL's active leader in career solo tackles (806) and second in total tackles (1,125) behind Seattle's Bobby Wagner. His 128 career tackles for loss is a huge number for someone whose primary contribution hasn't been pass-rushing, and with Thomas Davis retiring, no other active NFL player can match his career totals of both 12 interceptions and 24 sacks.

When Brady came to Tampa having known nothing but postseason success in his career, he saw how much his new teammates knew nearly the exact opposite and found motivation in wanting them to experience the joy of playoff football.

"A lot of guys on the team have never made the playoffs," Brady said. "I want them to experience that. It's an amazing part of being a professional player when you get to that time in the year. So much of the goals are about how do we put ourselves in a great position every week to be successful, and then obviously, over the course of the season, the more games you win, the better position you're in. … There's big goals for this team we put together. We really have a great opportunity."

Like Brooks, David has a chance to play his entire career for one team, and a trip to the Super Bowl helps his career move closer to Brooks as one of the few true icons in Bucs history. He will be an unrestricted free agent after the season, and while he could finish his career elsewhere as did other defensive leaders like Warren Sapp and John Lynch, he's made it clear he'd like to stay in Tampa.

Was this long-awaited Super Bowl run meant to happen for the Bucs? If you look closely at the logo for this year's Super Bowl logo, you see the L and the V on both sides of the Lombardi Trophy, which for some looks more like LIV. And that, of course, is David's jersey number, 54. ∎

Lavonte David's leadership and consistent presence on the Tampa Bay defense can't be overstated as one of the most important elements to the team's Super Bowl success.

BUCCANEERS 25, GIANTS 23

November 2, 2020 • East Rutherford, New Jersey

ESCAPE FROM NEW YORK

Bucs Squeak by Giants to Move to 6-2

By Joey Johnston

It was a cold and windy night at the Meadowlands. It was the bright lights of Monday Night Football, sure, but the stadium was empty. And the opponent was the one-win New York Giants.

For the Bucs, it was the recipe for a letdown and a hideous road defeat, just when their schedule was about to hit overdrive.

"In the past, we would've found a way to lose a game like that," Bucs wide receiver Mike Evans said.

Instead, the Bucs found a way to win, defeating the Giants 25-23 in a performance that posed more doubts than answered questions.

Place-kicker Ryan Succop was huge, connecting on field-goal attempts of 37, 40, 43 and 38 yards on a night when the offense found it difficult to finish.

"I've been on the opposite side of this hundreds of times, a bunch of times," Bucs linebacker Lavonte David said. "It's still good to be on the other side, get the win from it, even after an ugly football game.

"We didn't play our best at all, but it's something that we can still celebrate about because we got a win."

The Bucs (6-2), who tied the franchise's record for best eight-game starts (1979, 2002), fell behind 14-3 in the first half and were trailing heading to the fourth quarter. Quarterback Tom Brady threw a pair of touchdown passes, a 3-yarder to tight end Rob Gronkowski in the third quarter and an 8-yarder to Evans with 9:02 remaining that gave Tampa Bay the lead for good.

Two of the scoring plays were set up by interceptions from Carlton Davis and Sean Murphy-Bunting. And on both of those plays, there was duress created by pressure from linebacker Shaquil Barrett.

Still, it came down to the final minute. Giants quarterback Daniel Jones engineered a 13-play, 70-yard drive that included a pair of fourth-down conversions, including a 20-yard completion to Sterling Shephard on fourth-and-16. Three plays later, it was Jones to Golden Tate for a 19-yard score that pulled the Giants within 25-23.

On the two-point conversion, there was a collision between Giants running back Dion Lewis and Bucs rookie safety Antoine Winfield Jr. on Jones' pass attempt just inside the end zone. A flag was dropped. After a brief huddle of the officials, the flag was picked up.

Giants coach Joe Judge was incensed.

Bucs coach Bruce Arians was non-plused.

"The ball hit Antoine in the back," Arians said. "To me, there was no pass interference. I thought it was a good call. I don't know why it took so long."

Mike Evans hauls in a go-ahead touchdown in the fourth quarter, one of this five catches for 55 yards in the close win.

The Bucs had escaped.

But they never would have been in that winning position without Succop.

"It was kind of a tricky wind, but he's a veteran dude and that's what I love about him," Arians said. "He doesn't blink. He just goes out and gets his job done. He had a heck of a game. It's definitely a game-ball worthy game, that's for sure."

Succop's performance was a welcome change for what had been a place-kicking disaster for the Bucs. He's the ninth kicker since 2015, a veritable rogue's gallery that includes Matt Gay, Cairo Santos, Chandler Catanzaro, Patrick Murray, Nick Folk, Roberto Aguayo, Connor Barth and Kyle Brindza.

Clearly, eight wasn't enough. That crew combined to make 73.7 percent of their field-goal attempts (the NFL average was 83.9 during that span).

Aguayo, one of the best college kickers of all time at Florida State University, was a second-round pick in 2016. He was cut during 2017 training camp.

Gay was a fifth-round pick in 2019 but connected on just 77.1 percent of his field-goal attempts. He missed an extra point and a final-play 34-yarder in a 32-31 home loss against the Giants. He missed all three of his field-goal attempts — 49, 44 and 34 yards — in the season finale, a home overtime loss against the Atlanta Falcons.

So coming into the 2020 season, Arians had two obvious charges.

Reduce the turnovers.

And find someone who could make kicks, particularly those from reasonable range.

Succop, who had been 65-for-66 on field-goal attempts of 39 yards or shorter during his NFL career, was signed as a free-agent during training camp to compete with Gay. The decision was quickly made.

Succop became the kicker. Gay was cut, becoming the second drafted kicker in four seasons to be unceremoniously released.

Succop, meanwhile, was the final selection of the 2009 NFL Draft, the 256th pick overall, going to the Kansas City Chiefs. That earned him the title of "Mr. Irrelevant." But in his career with the Chiefs, Tennessee Titans and now Bucs, Succop has been nothing but relevant — and consistent.

"I always like to say, 'You're 0-for-0,'" Succop said. "Whatever you did last week, it doesn't matter. Whatever you did the week before that, it doesn't matter. The only thing that I focus on is the next kick — the one that's coming up — so I try to prepare each and every week to try and go out and give myself the best chance to kick well every time that my number is called. If you kick in this league long enough, there are going to be ups and downs."

His performance against the Giants was definitely an "up." He was recognized as NFC Special Teams Player of the Week. But even that award made him typically deferential.

"I think that Zach (Triner) and Bradley (Pinion) — our snapper and our punter and holder — those guys are doing such a great job," Succop said. "I give a lot of credit to them and the big boys up front. When you get an award like this, I always think of it as a team award."

But some things were undeniable. Succop has brought stability to place-kicking with the Bucs. With four made field goals against the Giants, he had 10 straight — and counting.

A reporter pointed that out to Arians.

"Don't jinx him, brother!" Arians said.

Spoken like a coach who had seen his share of errant field-goal attempts. With Succop's presence, the Bucs are no longer worrying about that. ∎

Kicker Ryan Succop was huge in the win over the Giants, hitting four field goals on four attempts.

SAINTS 38, BUCCANEERS 3
November 8, 2020 • Tampa, Florida

TOTAL COLLAPSE

Tampa Bay Lays a Prime-Time Egg in Loss to New Orleans

By Joey Johnston

It was supposed to be revenge.

It became a prime-time embarrassment.

New Orleans Saints 38, Bucs 3.

It was a reason to turn in early for the nation's fans of NBC's Sunday Night Football. At halftime, the Saints led 31-0. Only a 48-yard field goal by Ryan Succop with 5:52 remaining prevented the team's first shutout since 2012.

"It was shocking," Bucs coach Bruce Arians said.

The Bucs had a franchise-low five rushing attempts for 8 yards, while registering 194 total yards and going 1-for-9 on third-down conversions. Quarterback Tom Brady threw three interceptions and was sacked three times. Before the Bucs gained their initial first down, Saints quarterback Drew Brees had completed 14 of 16 passes for 145 yards and three touchdowns.

The Bucs (6-3), who lost 34-23 in the season-opener at New Orleans, fell a half-game behind the Saints (6-2) in the NFC South Division.

"Our offense, they couldn't get it going and it was just a total team collapse," Bucs linebacker Shaquil Barrett said. "That's not what we're about."

"Guys were (angry)," Bucs linebacker Lavonte David said. "You saw it on the sidelines. Guys were (angry) because we know we're that type of team, especially against a team who we obviously wanted to really beat. To go out there and put on a show like that on Sunday night … all you can do is move on from it."

Arians said he wondered if there was a recurring preparation theme for night games — losses against the Bears and Saints, plus a lackluster performance at the Giants.

"It's (starting the game with) three-and-out, then giving up a touchdown," Arians said. "I've got to do something in our preparation to change that, but I don't think our confidence is shaken.

"Learn from it. You don't bury your head in the sand. You own it. You go in, look at the tape, figure out what went right (and) what went wrong, then you move on to the next ballgame."

Before moving on, though, Brady refused to make excuses. Arians said the turnovers were a shared responsibility because there were dropped passes, leaky protection and misreads on patterns, along with some poor throws. It looked a lot like Tampa Bay's other (not for) prime-time performances.

"We need to perform better at any time," said Brady, who was 22 of 38 for 209 yards and a 40.4 passer rating, the third worst of his career in the regular season. "One o'clock, four o'clock, eight o'clock, Monday night, Sunday night — it doesn't matter. They're going to schedule the game and we're going to go out there and play. I don't really think it's anything magical that's happening. We've got to execute better and there are no excuses for what it is.

"We're going to get back to work and try to do

The Bucs did little right in the 38-3 thrashing by the Saints, their second loss to New Orleans of the season.

a lot better next week. We've got to win one game. We're 6-3. I wish we were a lot better than that, but that's where we're at."

There were no real bright spots for Tampa Bay, but it was the debut of heralded wide receiver Antonio Brown, who had three catches for 31 yards, although he had a miscommunication with Brady that led to one of the interceptions. As for the running game, well, it didn't exist.

"Offensively, we got out of that game plan so fast (that) I felt terrible for the left side of the line (protecting Brady's backside) because there was no threat of the run," Arians said. "I thought we had a really good plan for the running game, but when you go down 21-0, we tried to jump-start it with the two-minute drive just to get something going. It just didn't work. We got our (butts) kicked pretty good."

It was on to Carolina after a game that needed to be forgotten, even though it carried lessons that should always be remembered. ■

BUCCANEERS 46, PANTHERS 23
November 15, 2020 • Charlotte, North Carolina

TAKING FLIGHT

Patience Pays Off as Bucs Pull Away from Panthers in Bounceback Win

By Joey Johnston

In the shadow of his team's goalposts, backed to the 2-yard line, Bucs running back Ronald Jones broke through the line, juked past a safety and outran a linebacker.

He saw nothing but green grass.

He was soaring.

He was flying.

Which is more than his team could have said just 24 hours earlier.

When Jones raced for a 98-yard touchdown run in the third quarter, breaking open what became a 46-23 road victory against the Carolina Panthers, it was analogous to how the weekend evolved for Tampa Bay's players.

Frustrated, with patience running thin, the Bucs were grounded for the longest time. But they kept their cool. Eventually, they took flight.

After losing a mid-week practice day due to Hurricane Eta that swept through the Tampa Bay area, their Delta charter flight underwent interminable delays due to mechanical problems. Several hours later, the players disembarked because a new aircraft had been summoned.

So they hung out in the private terminal. The team ordered pizza and sandwiches. There were lots of card games. Finally, the Bucs took off and made it to their Charlotte, North Carolina, hotel about midnight — with a 1 p.m. kickoff looming.

Not ideal.

But the Bucs made it work.

"I can't say enough about our guys' focus," Bucs coach Bruce Arians said. "The first half, it wasn't our best defensive half. The second half was outstanding."

The Panthers jumped out early. The Bucs never led in the first half but managed a 17-17 tie at halftime on Tom Brady's 3-yard pass to wide receiver Mike Evans with 27 seconds to go before the break.

In the third quarter, Ryan Succop's opening-possession 24-yard field goal provided Tampa Bay's first lead at 20-17. It was still a skirmish. And things remained dicey when Carolina's Joseph Charlton boomed a 49-yard punt that was downed at Tampa Bay's 2-yard line.

On the first play, Jones got the call, hoping to wedge out some more territory. He got a lot more than that.

Jones, who had 23 carries for a career-high 192 yards (which tied for the fifth-best single-game total in franchise history), got past safety Tre Boston, then threw it in overdrive and roared around linebacker Jeremy Chinn, who dove and missed an ankle tackle.

Only four players in NFL history have a rushing attempt of 98 or more yards. Tony Dorsett (1983) and

Running back Ronald Jones breaks free for a 98-yard touchdown in the third quarter of the big win against the Panthers.

Derrick Henry (2018) have the record at 99 yards. Jones and Ahman Green (2003) went for 98.

"I've put on a little weight since college," Jones said. "The top-end speed is still there."

Indeed, the modern football landscape put Jones' run into proper perspective. The NFL's NextGen statistics indicated Jones ran at 21.19 mph — yep, that peak speed is really moving — and he broke free by peeking up at the Jumbotron.

"I could feel (Chinn)," said Jones, who started the game dismally, losing a first-quarter fumble that led to Carolina's first touchdown. "I probably shouldn't have looked at the Jumbotron, but it gave me an idea of where he was. I didn't know where the corners (were), so I just tried to go down the middle and change the angle on them."

After Jones' fumble, the Bucs (7-3) scored on their next nine possessions and outscored the Panthers 29-6 in the second half, surrendering only a 3-yard touchdown run by Teddy Bridgewater that was set up by Trenton Cannon's 98-yard kickoff return.

The defense held Carolina (3-7) to 187 total yards.

Meanwhile, the Bucs' offense produced 544 yards, including a sterling effort from quarterback Tom Brady (28 of 39, 341 yards, three touchdowns, one rushing score), Jones' head-turning afternoon and four field goals from Succop.

"We played better than we played last week obviously," said Brady, referring to a 38-3 home defeat against the New Orleans Saints. "And it's in there. We've just got to do it consistently and continue to make plays and run the ball like we ran it today."

Once the Bucs surged ahead, it was over. Todd Bowles' defense held the Panthers to 35 yards in the second half and 1-for-9 overall on third-down conversions.

"We basically said it was 0-0 (at halftime)," said Bucs linebacker Jason Pierre-Paul, whose key interception followed Jones' touchdown run, allowing Succop to kick another field goal and widen the margin. "That was basically it. We were just competing. I was competing."

Pierre-Paul also had one of the Bucs' three second-half sacks. It knocked out Bridgewater with a right-knee injury.

"Once we got the two-touchdown lead, the (Carolina) running game was going to be iffy at best," Arians said. "Our guys were just turning loose after the passer."

And the memories of a rough weekend finally dissipated.

"We can't fly a plane," Pierre-Paul said. "Only the pilot did and the captain can. But we made a bad situation into a great situation. Just winning this game today with my brothers made it even better. No matter what adversity throws at us, we're going to handle it pretty well and we did."

The Bucs traveled back to Tampa without incident, preparing for back-to-back home games against the NFL's elite, the Los Angeles Rams and Kansas City Chiefs.

How high could the Bucs fly?

They were about to find out. ∎

Mike Evans hauls in one of his six catches on the day, which went for a total of 77 yards and a touchdown.

RAMS 27, BUCCANEERS 24
November 23, 2020 • Tampa, Florida

STAGE FRIGHT

Tampa Bay Struggles Again Under the Lights, Drops Fourth of Season

By Joey Johnston

It happened again for the NFL's Not Ready For Prime Time Players — otherwise known as the Bucs.

With the nation watching on Monday Night Football, with a chance to get a foothold in the NFC playoff race, the Bucs short-circuited at Raymond James Stadium, falling 27-24 against the Los Angeles Rams.

Making matters worse, the Rams' winning margin occurred with 2:36 remaining on a 40-yard field goal by Matt Gay, the Bucs' fifth-round pick in 2019 who was cut during training camp. He had been signed by the Rams (7-3) in the previous week.

"You're sitting on the practice squad, and the first game you're going back to where you were last year and the place that you know you feel you should have been," Gay said. "You can't write it. It's one of those stories."

For the Bucs, it was the same old story.

When quarterback Tom Brady tried to pull it out — and add to his career total of 38 fourth-quarter comebacks — he misread the Rams' coverage and delivered a game-sealing interception into the waiting arms of rookie safety Jordan Fuller.

"At times, we look really, really good, and then there are times when we obviously don't," Bucs coach Bruce Arians said. "I felt very, very comfortable in the two-minute drive until that throw. We made some plays. Obviously, we didn't make enough in this ballgame — offense, defense or special teams — to win."

The Bucs (7-4), who fell one game-and-a-half behind the New Orleans Saints in the NFC South Division, moved to 1-3 in prime-time games. The day doesn't seem to matter — Monday, Sunday or even Thursday. When the lights come on, and the national-television cameras show up, the Bucs seemingly hit the snooze button.

Had the Bucs delivered a touchdown on the final drive, the narrative would have changed dramatically. Not this time. Brady (26 of 48, 216 yards, two touchdowns, two interceptions) was working from his 38-yard line, 1:57 left to play, one timeout remaining. On second down, he went deep for tight end Cameron Brate. But it was overshot — and right to Fuller.

"It was just a bad read," said Brady, whose team didn't offer much diversity (18 rushes for 42 yards, a 2.3-yard average). "Cameron was running up the seam and at the last second I saw the safety coming over and threw it over Cam's head. It was just a bad read and a bad throw, decision, everything."

Brady never hit any deep shots — the longest completion was 18 yards.

Rams quarterback Jared Goff used quick-rhythm passes to frustrate the Bucs. Goff was 39 of 51 for 376 yards and he had a pair of 100-yard receivers — Cooper Kupp (11 catches for 145 yards) and Robert Woods (12 for 130).

Two Goff passes in particular doomed the Bucs.

With 19 seconds remaining in the first half and the Rams out of timeouts in a 14-14 game, Goff found Woods on a 35-yard completion to the Tampa Bay 20-

The Bucs continued their inconsistent play, dropping to 7-4 on the season and 1-3 in prime-time games.

yard line. Goff hustled to the line and spiked it, allowing Gay to hit a 38-yard field goal as time elapsed.

Later, Goff made a huge mistake when the Rams led by one touchdown midway through the fourth quarter. Safety Jordan Whitehead intercepted at the Ram 44-yard line and gave the Bucs life. Finishing a seven-play, 44-yard drive, Brady found Chris Godwin, who dove over the right pylon for a 13-yard touchdown and it was tied with 3:53 remaining.

The Bucs were promptly deflated on a dagger, Goff's 19-yard toss to Kupp on third-and-1 from Tampa Bay's

43. Gay connected on the go-ahead field goal. There was ample time, but Brady uncharacteristically didn't have the big-game comeback formula.

And the Bucs' postseason quest got more challenging.

"Every game is like a playoff game," Whitehead said. "That's the mentality we have to take into the next game. We've got another tough one."

Layups weren't immediately available. The Bucs, in desperate need of a confidence boost, were now bracing for the Kansas City Chiefs, the defending Super Bowl champions. ■

CHIEFS 27, BUCCANEERS 24
November 29, 2020 • Tampa, Florida

SLIDING INTO THE BYE

Bucs Enter Much-Needed Bye-Week with Third Loss in Four Games

By Joey Johnston

After another painfully close outcome, a 27-24 heartbreaking loss against the powerful Kansas City Chiefs at Raymond James Stadium, the Bucs were ready for the bye-week break.

A break from the rigorous competition after losing three of their last four games.

A break from the pattern of falling behind early.

And a break from the expectations.

"Everybody tried to hand us the Lombardi Trophy in August," Bucs coach Bruce Arians said. "You don't just throw guys out there with names. You've got to practice. You've got to learn to get in sync with each other. That takes time."

But are the Bucs (7-5) running out of time?

They are clinging to the NFC's final playoff spot — by their fingernails — and have a favorable remaining schedule. It wouldn't be a stretch for the Chiefs (10-1), defending world champions, to return here for Super Bowl LV on Feb. 7.

Can the Bucs make it a rematch? Maybe. But there's work to do — lots of it.

The three-point margin against the Chiefs was a bit of an optical illusion. Quarterback Tom Brady threw fourth-quarter touchdown passes of 31 and 7 yards to wide receiver Mike Evans, the last coming with 4:10 remaining and momentum had seemingly shifted.

But the Bucs never got the ball back. Chiefs quarterback Patrick Mahomes played keep-away, a departure from the scorching first half, when he passed for 359 of his 462 yards (on 37 of 49 passing). You practically needed dental records to identify members of the Bucs' secondary.

The Bucs mostly opted for man-to-man coverage on the human blur, wide receiver Tyreek Hill. That man was cornerback Carlton Davis. The Bucs paid dearly for that strategy.

Hill finished with 13 catches for 269 yards — the most receiving yards ever allowed to a player by the Bucs. Hill had touchdown receptions of 75, 44 and 20 yards, punctuating the 44-yarder by stopping at the goal line and doing a back flip into the end zone.

Hill had an unthinkable seven catches for 203 yards in the first quarter, when the Chiefs bolted to a 17-0 advantage. Slow start for the Bucs? Yes, once again. The Bucs, who have been outscored 49-7 in the first quarter of the last four games, had just one first down in their initial four possessions.

Ronald Jones had 66 yards rushing on just nine carries to go along with a 37-yard touchdown reception, but it wasn't enough to beat the defending champions.

Brady heated up, finishing 27 of 41 for 345 yards and three touchdowns. But he also had two second-half interceptions, both in Kansas City territory.

"We battled back," Brady said. "We unfortunately left ourselves with a big deficit. We've got to make the plays that are there. We've got to do our job, stay on the field and keep them off the field."

That just couldn't happen against Mahomes.

"Very, very few guys that I've seen in this league or any league who can backpedal 8, 9, 10, 11 yards in the pocket and throw a dime 25 yards down the field," Arians said. "And he can read the defense as he does it. That makes him more explosive."

The Chiefs entered the fourth quarter with a 17-point lead and held the ball for nearly 10 minutes on their final two possessions without scoring. That was the idea.

"I learned a long time ago, you don't give Tom Brady another shot," Chiefs coach Andy Reid said. "That's why he's the G.O.A.T. (Greatest Of All Time). So don't give them the ball back."

As the season enters the final quadrant, despite dropping three consecutive home games, Arians said he remains confident if the Bucs follow a preferred strategy.

"First and foremost, get healthy and beat the virus," Arians said. "Every team that has come back from the bye has had a virus problem. We can't finish our season with eight, nine or 10 guys staying home.

"Every game is a big game — 11-5 will do it. One at a time." ∎

Kansas City quarterback Patrick Mahomes prevailed over Tom Brady in this matchup, but an even bigger stage awaited the two in Super Bowl LV.

BUCCANEERS 26, VIKINGS 14

December 13, 2020 • Tampa, Florida

SWAGGER'S BACK

Bucs Dispatch Vikings, Get Back on the Winning Track

By Joey Johnston

The Bucs are hunting for their first postseason in berth in 13 years.

Appropriately, Tampa Bay's pass-rushers went hunting for the quarterback at Raymond James Stadium and that established the momentum of a pivotal 26-14 victory against the Minnesota Vikings.

The Bucs (8-5) had lost three of their last four games heading into their bye week. Dropping a game against the Vikings (6-7), who came in winning five of their last six contests, might have jeopardized the Bucs' chances in the NFC power structure.

The Vikings were game opponents. Dalvin Cook powered for 102 yards against the NFL's No. 1-ranked rushing defense. The Vikings nearly doubled up the Bucs in time of possession.

But the Bucs registered six sacks against Vikings quarterback Kirk Cousins, and most were critical.

Two Viking drives that reached the Bucs' 11- and 8-yard line were thwarted by third-down sacks and that was bad news for Minnesota's suddenly unreliable place-kicker, Dan Bailey, who missed attempts of 36, 54 and 46 yards (along with an extra-point try).

Minnesota's first drive reached the Tampa Bay 32, but the Vikings were forced to punt after a sack. And the Vikings' last-gasp fourth-quarter drive ended with a strip sack (sound familiar?) by linebacker Jason Pierre-Paul.

It was an especially satisfying two-sack afternoon for Shaquil Barrett, the other pass-rushing linebacker. Barrett, a free-agent signing, had a breakout season in 2019 with an NFL-leading 19.5 sacks. His sack totals have been less consistent this season, coming more in spurts. His performance against the Vikings was a high point.

"We were most definitely ready to feast and get after the quarterback once we were up by double digits with a certain amount of time left," said Barrett, who has shifted to the right side where he seems to be more comfortable. "We knew they had to pass, and we were ready to take advantage of it.

"I started slow and I just have to pick it up. I want to do my job as much as possible and be known as one of the best. So in order to do that, you have to have the stats. You have to have the numbers to go with it."

In all the Vikings had five drives inside the Bucs' 40-yard line that produced no points.

It was rookie safety Antoine Winfield Jr. and Barrett who came up big on the game's pivotal drive, when the Vikings opened the third quarter trying to chip into Tampa Bay's 17-6 advantage.

Minnesota wouldn't go away, reaching the Bucs' 8-yard line. On second down, the blitzing Winfield took down Cousins with a 12-yard loss. Then it was Barrett breaking through and trapping Cousins for a 9-yard sack.

Antoine Winfield Jr. (31) sacks and strips the ball from Minnesota Vikings quarterback Kirk Cousins (8) during Tampa Bay's 26-14 win.

Enter Bailey, who missed for a third occasion, this time from 46 yards.

For Winfield, a second-round rookie from the University of Minnesota whose father once played for the Vikings, it was another eye-opening performance. In addition to his sack, he had 11 tackles and a forced fumble.

"He (Winfield) and Tristan (Wirfs, right tackle) should be hitting the proverbial 'rookie wall' by now," Bucs coach Bruce Arians said. "But those kids, they're mature beyond their years, especially in football acumen. Antoine is just so heady. He has his dad to lean on. He has all his coaches to lean on. And he puts the time in.

"I'm sure he's elated (and his) family is probably elated. When you play the team you grew up watching your dad (play for) and (remember) being in the locker room, it's huge."

Tampa Bay's aggressive defense was a good compliment to its efficient offense.

Because of Minnesota's time-of-possession dominance, the Bucs had limited opportunities, but made good use of them. The Bucs had no turnovers and quarterback Tom Brady (15 of 23, 196 yards) was not sacked.

Brady had a pair of touchdown passes, a 48-yarder to wide receiver Scotty Miller and a 2-yarder to tight end Rob Gronkowski in the third quarter that put the Bucs up 23-6.

But the biggest Brady-to-Gronkowski connection actually didn't connect. With one second remaining in the first half, Brady tried a Hail Mary to the end zone and drew a 46-yard pass-interference call on Minnesota. Place-kicker Ryan Succop punched in a tack-on 18-yard field goal that deflated the Vikings.

Ronald Jones rushed for 80 yards, but the bigger story was the use of LeSean "Shady" McCoy, inactive through most of the season, who carried four times for 32 yards. Leonard Fournette, the other running back, did not dress for the game.

"I love Leonard," Arians said. "I think he's a heck of a kid and a great player. We just wanted to get 'Shady' back involved. He's fresh and he showed it today. I took the risk and he made it pay off. He made the best of his opportunity."

So did the Bucs.

By defeating the Vikings, they diminished the playoff chances of another NFC rival and assured themselves of a head-to-head tiebreaker. It wasn't perfect, but it was a needed performance heading down the stretch.

If nothing else, with everything still on the line, Arians regained some swagger.

"It was huge," Arians said. "We had to do this. I was asked early this week about our identity. I think we just showed it. We can do any damn thing we want to do." ∎

Ronald Jones picked up 80 yards and a touchdown on 18 carries in Tampa Bay's post bye-week win over the Vikings.

87

TIGHT END

ROB GRONKOWSKI

Rested and Refreshed, Gronk Brings Good Vibes On and Off the Field

By Greg Auman

As you might have expected, Rob Gronkowski was enjoying retirement.

The former Patriots tight end was only 30, and like Bucs coach Bruce Arians, health had played a major role in his decision to retire. He had gingerly walked away after another Super Bowl championship, and in a year away from football, he had dabbled as an NFL studio analyst, a professional wrestler and even on prime-time TV celebrity game shows.

But when Tom Brady signed with the Bucs in March, it begged the question: Would his best target from his New England days join him for a second chapter of his own in Tampa? Gronkowski had caught 78 touchdown passes from Brady, twice as much as the quarterback's next closest teammate, and even while sitting out 2019, he had caught more touchdowns than any other NFL player in the 2010s.

The answer, just before the NFL Draft in April? Of course he was. The Bucs sent a fourth-round pick to the Patriots to acquire Gronkowski's rights, paying him the $10 million he was due on his old contract in New England. And a passing combo that was part of five Super Bowls and three championships was reunited, going after another ring in Tampa.

"Playing with Tom is special," Gronkowski said on his introductory video call with reporters. "He's one of the greatest quarterbacks of all time. To build a connection with a quarterback, too, is something special. You've seen it many times with many other players. They switch teams and they might not have the same chemistry as with one of their other quarterbacks. We have a great chemistry out there, and every time we get together, it's like the old days. It doesn't matter if we take a month off, or six months apart."

Despite that, it was a quiet start for Gronkowski. With a wealth of talented options for Brady to throw to, Gronkowski had 11 receiving yards in his debut, and then zero catches on zero targets the next week.

"I'm a blocking tight end," he said, a subtle smile on his face. "I'm here to block, baby."

Three more games would pass without a touchdown, and Bucs fans still hadn't seen the famous "Gronk spike" to celebrate a touchdown. Green Bay came to town in Week 6, and after an early 10-0 deficit,

Rob Gronkowski lived up to his reputation as a player and personality for the Bucs, producing in big moments on the field and keeping things loose in the locker room and with teammates.

the Bucs exploded for 28 points in the second quarter, the final touchdown just before the half soundly so familiar: Brady to Gronkowski.

Gronkowski scored touchdowns in three straight games, and the chemistry was there with Brady again. The two did a weekly video short for the Bucs' official website called "The Tommy and Gronky Show," the two in sunglasses and sandals, a plastic swimming pool between them, flanked by flamingoes and ferns, two old pals trading jokes in the Florida sun.

Gronkowski added two more touchdowns in a December rout of the Lions, giving him seven to tie for the team lead over the final 11 games of the regular season. What's more, he finished the regular season without missing a single game, doing so for the first time since 2011.

His time in New England had been marked by so many injuries — back surgeries, concussions, a pulmonary contusion and injuries to his hamstring, groin and thigh. Before the season, an online sports book had gone so far as to set the over-under on how many games Gronkowski would miss at 4.5. This was that rare time to take the under with him.

As the playoffs began, Gronkowski showed what a complete tight end is, shifting into a different role as an extra blocker and protector for Brady. He really was a blocking tight end, again with no catches in the playoff win at Washington, with just one catch for 14 yards in the win at New Orleans.

Brady hadn't forgotten about him though, and with the game on the line in the fourth quarter in Green Bay, the Bucs called a trick play of sorts, faking an end-around to receiver Scotty Miller, then faking a screen to him, with Brady turning around and throwing a screen to Gronkowski, who rumbled 29 yards, putting the Bucs in position for a 46-yard field goal to extend their lead to eight points.

In the end, it didn't take much for Gronkowski to embrace his inner Florida Man — "I'm a T-shirt and shorts guy, rolling out of bed with the sandals," he said in April. Like Brady, his past accomplishments set the standard for success impossibly high, and yet he helped the Bucs do that by reaching the Super Bowl.

"It has matched a lot of hopes that I had coming here big time," Gronkowski said. "It's just so hard to win football games in the NFL. Week in and week out, it's just hard to win games. The main goal, obviously, is always to make it to the Super Bowl, but it's hard. It's one of the hardest things to do out there in the sports world. Expectations — really, that's all, is to give it your all. Obviously you want to win games and the main goal is to win it all, but to just be where we are now is just unbelievable. It's exceptional. I feel like it's well-deserved overall as an organization. Everyone has been working hard. Everyone has been putting their time in. Overall, it's been a great experience. I'm not surprised that we're this far, but at the same time, I know how hard it is to get this far and how much work gets put in."

Gronkowski's contract is up after this one season in Tampa, but with the postseason success the Bucs had, he said he wanted to play another year with Brady and the Bucs. Healthy again and winning again, this was a comeback to savor. And for his new teammates, the Gronk experience was special as well.

"If you're having a bad day, I suggest any of you just go spend a little time with Gronk," general manager Jason Licht said. "He just lifts you up just by being with him. He's funny — we have conversations every day and I look forward to it. I tell my wife, 'I can't wait to go talk to Gronk at practice today.' He's just being himself, he's very authentic, he loves the game and when it's time to be serious, he's very serious. There's a lot of talk about what Tom has done for this locker room — and it's all warranted — but what Gronk has done for this locker room is equally as amazing. Just a great teammate and loves life." ■

Rob Gronkowski started the season slow but eventually came on, rekindling the connection he had with longtime teammate Tom Brady.

BUCCANEERS 31, FALCONS 27
December 20, 2020 • Atlanta, Georgia

GLASS-HALF-FULL

Bucs Overcome First-Half Struggles for Dominant Finish, Comeback Win

By Joey Johnston

For 30 glorious minutes, it was a sideline-to-sideline symposium on just how good the Bucs could become.

The offense was explosive, efficient and fun. The defense was menacing, relentless and unyielding.

It wasn't half-bad at all.

That was the uneven story of the Bucs' electrifying 31-27 victory against the Atlanta Falcons at Mercedes-Benz Stadium. It was a glass-half-full performance — as in the second half, when the Bucs were practically unstoppable.

Still, the Bucs (9-5), who clinched their first winning season since 2016 and came to the brink of their first playoff appearance since 2007, continued to confound. The Falcons (4-10) led 17-0 at halftime. And the sputtering start continued another wheel-spinning trend for the Bucs, who have been outscored 59-7 in the first quarter of their last six games.

"The second half was the way we're capable of playing, the way we should be playing," Bucs coach Bruce Arians said. "My comments to the team after the game were, 'If we can play 30 minutes like that, why the hell can't we play 60?'

"And it's frustrating. We lost to the Chiefs and Rams by three, both of those games playing this way. And it's not going to happen. We're not going to beat good teams playing this way. We've got to play better in the first half than we played today."

Point taken, Coach.

But, oh, that second half …

It culminated when Bucs quarterback Tom Brady delivered a 46-yard touchdown pass to wide receiver Antonio Brown (his first Tampa Bay score) with 6:19 remaining to provide their first lead of the afternoon.

Overall, Brady finished 31 of 45 for 390 yards and two touchdowns. He also helped the Bucs score on five straight possessions after halftime (four touchdowns and a field goal) — a 31-point blitz that also included a pair of scoring runs from Leonard Fournette, a 4-yard touchdown pass to Chris Godwin and a 27-yard field goal by Ryan Succop.

For the Falcons, who briefly regained the lead on a 52-yard field goal by Younghoe Koo with 8:22 remaining before the Brady-to-Brown connection restored order, it was a demoralizing defeat.

But not THE demoralizing defeat. That was the 2017 Super Bowl, when the Falcons were beaten 34-28 in overtime by the New England Patriots. The Falcons led 28-3 midway through the third quarter before New England's comeback was administered by … Tom Brady.

On this afternoon, after a second-half trade of touchdowns, the Falcons led 24-7 midway through

Tom Brady threw for 390 yards and two touchdowns, outdueling the Falcons and their fellow veteran quarterback, Matt Ryan.

the third quarter before Tampa Bay's comeback was administered by … Tom Brady.

In the second half alone, Brady was 21 of 29 for 320 yards. It was the fourth-highest single-half passing total in franchise history. And in a way, it wasn't that surprising.

"He's just a winner," Arians said. "He knows how to do it. Tom has always been a fourth-quarter player."

"A lot of it is his track record (and) the belief he kind of inspires in all of us," Bucs tight end Cameron Brate said. "He has done it on the biggest stage — the 28-3 game. We've seen him do it and we just have a ton of confidence in him. He puts that confidence in us as well. There was really no panic in the locker room."

Brady spread around the credit like he was picking from his fleet of receivers.

"It was great poise by everybody," Brady said. "Everybody hung in there. We got off to a tough start but found a way to win."

For Brady, it was particularly rewarding that Brown, an oft-troubled veteran brought in at mid-season, was on the receiving end of Tampa Bay's game-winning pass.

"He has done a lot of work to get to this point," Brady said.

When Brown reached the end zone, he dropped to his knees and raised his arms to the sky.

"It has been a long journey for me," Brown said. "He (Brady) hit me right in the numbers. (I'm) extremely grateful to be here with Tampa Bay and have the opportunity live out my dream and play football."

Brown made it happen at the key moment, but it took a lot more. Brady utilized 10 different receivers, including Mike Evans (six catches for 110 yards), Brown (five for 93) and Brate (four for 54) leading the way.

The defense couldn't be overlooked either — particularly middle linebacker Devin White, who had 12 tackles and three sacks (all in the fourth quarter). In the second half, the Falcons were limited to 108 yards and 0-for-5 on third-down conversions.

With the game tied 24-24, Bucs rookie safety Antoine Winfield Jr. deflected an end-zone pass that looked like a touchdown to wide receiver Calvin Ridley. Then White's third-and-6 takedown of Falcons quarterback Matt Ryan forced Koo's field-goal attempt.

White had two more sacks of Ryan deep in Falcons territory that sealed the comeback victory.

"He's so quick," Arians said of White. "When he sees the gap, man, he can shoot it. He got him (Ryan) on the ground three times. They were big, big sacks."

White said he was inspired by the halftime words of defensive coordinator Todd Bowles, who urged him to take over the game.

"I just played instinct football," White said. "I want to help my defense get off the field and give us a lot more energy to finish the game."

The start wasn't good, but the finish was tremendous. It wasn't completely what the Bucs wanted as the playoffs approached, but it wasn't half-bad, either. ∎

Running back Leonard Fournette had 49 yards and two touchdowns on 14 carries in the road win over the Falcons.

ROOKIES IN NAME ONLY

Antoine Winfield Jr. and Tristan Wirfs Prove to be Quick and Valuable Learners

By Greg Auman

On a team loaded with seasoned veterans and established stars, the Bucs still found room to get every-down impacts from rookies on both sides of the ball, in their top two draft picks, tackle Tristan Wirfs and safety Antoine Winfield Jr.

"They've been fantastic," coach Bruce Arians said during the Bucs' playoff run. "Tristan and Antoine, I really don't consider them rookies anymore. With how many games they've played, they're in their sophomore year, almost to the end of it."

Both stepped in so immediately as reliable starters that it's hard to imagine Tampa Bay without them. Wirfs, the team's first-round pick out of Iowa, was the only Bucs player on the field for every single offensive snap — 1,073 of them — allowing a single sack all year, playing another 88 on special teams. Winfield, the second-round pick from Minnesota, had the most snaps of any defensive rookie in the entire league with 1,034, adding another 84 on special teams and still not committing a single penalty.

Both players were named to the Pro Football Writers Association's All-Rookie Team, and Wirfs finished third among NFL right tackles in All-Pro voting, making 10 of 50 ballots.

Wirfs was widely seen as one of the top four tackles in this year's draft, with a rare athleticism for a prospect his size. A viral video showed him explosive enough that, standing in a pool, he could jump entirely out of the water at 300-plus pounds. The Bucs, picking at No. 14 overall, liked him enough that they were willing to give up a fourth-round pick to move up one spot with the 49ers, making sure they got him at No. 13 overall.

The Bucs felt fortunate that Winfield was still available with the 45th overall pick in the second round. They had scouted him in person on his future home field, Raymond James Stadium, when Minnesota played in the Outback Bowl and beat Auburn, with the help of the Bucs' fifth-round pick, receiver Tyler Johnson.

Winfield followed in the footsteps of his father, Antoine Winfield Sr., who played 14 years in the NFL as an undersized, playmaking cornerback, amassing 27 interceptions, including one off Tom Brady, his son's ageless new teammate. The two talked every day, going over film together, father helping son with how to read offenses and learn tendencies of players he was covering. He showed an instinct for being around the ball from the very beginning, as he was the NFL's Defensive Rookie of the Month for September.

"I would say it's natural, but it also comes with a lot

Antoine Winfield Jr. took after his father Antoine Winfield Sr., a terrific NFL defensive back over 14 years in his own right, as Winfield Jr. quickly adapted to the pro game and excelled.

of hard work," Winfield said of his stellar start. "If you do it in practice, you'll do it in the game, so my goal is always to stay around the ball in practice. Then, it shows up during game time. You have to practice it all the time for it to actually happen."

He created a spark in the Bucs' first win of the season, against Carolina in Week 2, blitzing quarterback Teddy Bridgewater and forcing a sack that was recovered by teammate Jason Pierre-Paul. He got another sack the following week in a win against Denver, then got his first NFL interception in the Bucs' win at Las Vegas. When the Giants scored a touchdown to pull within a two-point conversion of tying the Bucs in Week 8, it was Winfield who broke up the pass on the conversion — a flag was thrown for pass interference, then picked up after a moment — and sealed another Bucs win.

Winfield's biggest play came in the postseason, as he punched the ball loose from Saints tight end Jared Cook for a key turnover as the Bucs rallied to beat the Saints in New Orleans to advance to the NFC Championship Game. He would miss that game in Green Bay with an ankle injury, his absence felt and appreciated for the first time.

Wirfs, at the same time, stood out by the complete absence of plays allowed by opposing pass-rushers. Bucs run game coordinator Harold Goodwin, who oversees the offensive line, said in December that Wirfs had exceeded his expectations, even as a first-round pick who came in with a sterling reputation, comparing him to Steelers center Maurkice Pouncey, who has been to nine straight Pro Bowls.

"Obviously, he's a special rookie," Goodwin said. "Probably the last special one I've been around was Maurkice Pouncey, just to come in and be a Day 1 starter type of guy, to excel at a high level from a playing standpoint, has been awesome. I've been shocked,

especially with all the guys he's been against from a pass-rush standpoint. He's held up pretty good. Obviously, we've talked before about that one hiccup against Khalil Mack, but other than that, he's been phenomenal."

Both came to the Bucs with a poise and maturity you don't expect from first-year players. The two Bucs have acted like rookies so infrequently that those rare moments have been amusing. In a Week 14 win against the Vikings, tight end Rob Gronkowski scored a touchdown and began his signature "Gronk spike," but did it directly towards an oncoming Wirfs, who flinched big-time and caught all kinds of grief from his teammates.

"You know, with a football," he said, "you never know what way it's going to bounce, so I was just protecting."

And that's what he did, all year long. ■

Offensive tackle Tristan Wirfs (78) was the rare model of consistency as a rookie, as he didn't miss a single offensive snap all season.

BUCCANEERS 47, LIONS 7
December 26, 2020 • Detroit, Michigan

PLAYOFF BOUND!

Tampa Bay Ends 13-Year Playoff Drought in Romp Over Detroit

By Joey Johnston

For Bucs wide receiver Mike Evans, it had been seven seasons of sustained individual excellence — but nothing resembling a championship.

"We've been scratching and clawing every single year to try to make the tournament," Evans said.

For Bucs defensive lineman William Gholston, it had been eight seasons of frustration. And now he was in his hometown of Detroit with a chance to do something special.

"I was thinking about the first time I got on Ford Field," Gholston said. "I was in little league, a PAL (Police Athletic League) All-Star practice. I think I was 11 or 12."

For Bucs linebacker Lavonte David, it had been nine seasons of grinding, a largely anonymous quest where national recognition was elusive and losing teams were commonplace.

"Everybody knows what it took," David said. "A lot of guys, staff, everybody was like, 'It's about time.' They said they're proud of me. They're happy for me."

For the Bucs (10-5), it was a jubilant locker room, the end of a 13-year playoff drought and, of course, lots and lots of happiness. That quality — happiness — is relative. For Bucs quarterback Tom Brady, who has six Super Bowl rings and two decades of glory, just making the playoffs probably wasn't enough reason for a parade.

"There will be a bunch of teams that make it to the playoffs this year and there's only going to be one team that ends up happy," Brady said. "We're not done."

When the Bucs defeated the Detroit Lions 47-7, blasting a team (5-10) that was without its interim head coach (Darrell Bevell, COVID-19 protocol) and its quarterback (Matthew Stafford, lower-leg injury on the first series), there was a lack of suspense.

But no one apologized for a result that resembled a scrimmage in the cavernous empty stadium one day after Christmas.

The Bucs, who had been outscored 59-7 in the first quarter of their last six games, produced touchdowns on their initial two possessions and led 34-0 at halftime (with 410 total yards). They finished with a franchise-record 588 total yards. For the third straight game, the Bucs didn't have a turnover.

Brady played only the first half, going 22 of 27 for 348 yards and four touchdowns. So including the second half of Tampa Bay's preceding game at Atlanta, these were the four-quarter totals for Brady — 43 of 56 (76.8 completion percentage) for 668 yards and six touchdowns.

"Tom is a pretty special player," Bucs coach Bruce Arians deadpanned.

And making the playoffs?

Wide receiver Antonio Brown (81) celebrates a second quarter touchdown, one of his four catches for 35 yards in the win over the Lions.

Also pretty special.

"It means the world," Arians said. "This is why you coach. You want to get a chance to win a championship. Ever since I've gotten to Tampa, we've never had to ask our guys to work hard. We've gotten smarter. We've gotten more disciplined. And it's starting to show."

The acquisition of Brady will be the most tangible evidence of Tampa Bay's graduation to the postseason, but Arians said the foundation already was in place.

"It was putting the secondary together first," Arians said. "We needed a defense if we were going to win. I knew we'd score points. We've always scored points. It's just a matter of getting a defense. We wanted to keep all those (defensive) guys here.

"Then just add pieces offensively. Obviously, Tom (Brady) was huge. Rob (Gronkowski) was huge. They were more, 'We know how to win.' That's what they brought. I like where we're at now. Anything can happen. I've been a six seed (with the Steelers) and won the Super Bowl. Anything's possible. Now that we're in the dance, we're going to see what next week brings and where we're going."

Besides the act of solidifying their postseason position, the Bucs' next week (regular-season finale, home game against the Atlanta Falcons), figures to be a major opportunity for Evans, who can become the first player in NFL history to register 1,000-yard receiving seasons in each of his first seven years.

Evans, who had 10 catches for 181 yards and two touchdowns against the Lions, needs 40 yards to achieve the milestone.

"I desperately want that to happen," Arians said. "Whatever he needs, I'm sure Atlanta's not going to want to give it to him, so we'll have to find some creative ways to get it for him."

Beating Atlanta for the 11th win is everyone's priority on the Bucs. After that, though, helping Evans reach an individual milestone is important.

"They care about me, and I appreciate that a lot," Evans said. "They definitely want me to get the record (and) to be the first in NFL history. It's a huge accomplishment. I'm just appreciative that they care about me like that and that they want me to get it."

Evans has 13 touchdowns, breaking his own single-season record. And he has another distinction, becoming the first player in NFL history with at least 8,000 receiving yards and at least 60 receiving touchdowns in his first seven seasons.

"Early in the season, I was hurt really bad, but it's my job to play," Evans said. "I'm getting back on track, getting healthier, but we definitely as a team have just been battling injuries. We're trending up right now, so we're happy about that."

Happiness.

It was all around in the Bucs' locker room. It was a moment to savor, a snapshot to relish. But not for long.

As Brady said, they weren't done. ∎

Tyler Johnson fends off Lions safety Tracy Walker on a 35-yard catch, his lone grab on the day.

BUCCANEERS 44, FALCONS 27

January 3, 2021 • Tampa, Florida

ON TO THE BIG STAGE

Tampa Bay Overcomes Health Scares, Looks Ahead to Postseason After Beating Atlanta

By Joey Johnston

On an afternoon when the socially distanced fans got to celebrate their postseason-ready Bucs, there were a few scares that surfaced during a regular-season ending 44-27 victory against the Atlanta Falcons.

Wide receiver Mike Evans, just one play after a 20-yard reception made him the first player in NFL history with seven consecutive 1,000-yard seasons to begin a career, he was injured during a freak end-zone slip. The turf seemed to give way and Evans was carted off to the locker room with a left knee injury.

Later, the Bucs (11-5) reported there was no structural damage to Evans' knee, and he had an opportunity to play in the NFC Wild-Card Round against the Washington Football Team (7-9), champions of a depleted NFC East Division.

The news wasn't as good for Bucs middle linebacker Devin White, the team's leading tackler who didn't play due to COVID-19. Because of timing protocols, he won't be eligible to play in the opening postseason game at Washington.

White was replaced by Kevin Minter, whose nine tackles led the Bucs.

"This is kind of what we do, right?" Minter said. "Coach (Bruce Arians) always talks about 'next man up' and that's something we live by in this locker room. Regardless of who's down, there are no excuses.

"We're all Bucs and we've all got goals in mind. We're trying to get that championship. So regardless of who's playing, you need to strap the helmet on and go. And I'll be damned if I'm the one that let my team down."

That was also the philosophy at receiver.

The Bucs' touted depth wasn't just talk. It was real. Against the Falcons (4-12), despite the jarring sight of Evans getting hurt, the Bucs got winning performances from Antonio Brown (11 catches, 138 yards, two touchdowns) and Chris Godwin (five catches, 133 yards, two touchdowns).

Regardless of who was on the receiving end, quarterback Tom Brady was again on his A-game, completing 26 of 41 passes for 399 yards and four touchdowns.

After Falcons quarterback Matt Ryan hit tight end Hayden Hurst on a 1-yard touchdown with 8:19 remaining, cutting the Bucs' lead to 30-27, Brady went back to work. He engineered an eight-play, 75-yard touchdown drive that culminated with a 4-yard pass to Godwin. When defensive back Sean Murphy-Bunting recovered a Falcon fumble, it took Brady only three plays to produce a 30-yard scoring pass to Brown.

Brady finished the regular season with a franchise-record 40 touchdown passes, the second-highest total of his career (behind 50 in 2007). He also had a franchise-best 102.2 passer rating for the season, while finishing with 4,633 yards, the second-most in franchise history (5,109 yards by Jameis Winston in 2019).

"Whatever happens for me as a quarterback is reflective of what we do as an offense," Brady said. "I love playing with the guys I play with. We've got a great group of receivers, a great group of tight ends, very selfless. The

The Bucs took care of the Falcons for the second time in three weeks, giving them four consecutive wins heading into the playoffs.

backs have done an incredible job, and the offensive line has been playing great."

And for anyone who believed Brady's season was typically brilliant, an expectation for the mortal-lock Pro Football Hall of Famer, Arians provided some perspective.

"When we first met (after Brady signed with the Bucs), that's really what we talked about," Arians said. "The players we had and what he could do with the players we have. I envisioned 40 (touchdowns). I really did. When (Brady) first signed, it was like, 'OK, we'll be a 40 (touchdowns) and 10 (interceptions) team.

"But I was expecting practice. I was expecting (organized team activities) and everything else (that was negated by COVID-19). But what he has done with none of that? Especially this last half of the season, it's incredible."

So was the accomplishment by Evans. Even with the emotional shock of his injury, it didn't diminish the respect shown by players and coaches.

"It's definitely a roller coaster of emotions," Godwin said. "He breaks the record, and I was so proud just

of the man that Mike is and the way he works. Then he goes down. It hurts. I think the life in the stadium got sucked out of it, and I think that's when you see how important Mike really is to this team, to the organization, to this city."

"It's an incredible record to have," Brady said. "Toughness, dependability. Obviously, skill. But attitude plays a big factor into those things. I just love playing with the guy. When he went out (of the game), other guys kept making plays. So we've got to keep it going. Now that the regular season is over, it's one football game. Who executes when the pressure is on?"

After some shaky moments — including losing three of four games heading into December — the Bucs appear to be peaking.

"We're starting to see the fruits of our labor," Godwin said. "I think we're getting the right play calls at the right time and we're executing so much better. I think you are starting to see just how much talent we really have."

"We obviously have to sharpen some things up, especially on defense," Minter said. "But we're going into this thing knowing that we can beat anybody." ■

13
WIDE RECEIVER

MIKE EVANS

Record-Breaking Season for Evans a Testament to His Consistently Elite Presence on the Bucs

By Greg Auman

It was an obscure record to chase, but it spoke volumes of the constant, reliable presence Mike Evans has been in his NFL career.

In each of his first six years with the Bucs, Evans had topped 1,000 receiving yards, and the only other player in NFL history to do so at the start of his career was Pro Football Hall of Fame receiver Randy Moss. If he did it again in 2020, he'd have the record all to himself.

Evans had pushed through injuries, had drawn extra coverage from opponents, but with three games left in the season, Evans had just 669 receiving yards, and it looked like the wealth of talented options for Tom Brady to throw to would end his streak at six straight seasons.

Evans was focused on ending another career-long streak — six years and no playoff appearances — but even coach Bruce Arians spoke about how important it was to help get him to 1,000 yards.

"I desperately want that to happen," said Arians, wanting to give Evans a small piece of history.

Sure enough, Evans had six catches for 110 yards in a win against the Falcons, and in a 47-7 rout of the Lions, he had 10 catches for 181 yards and two touchdowns, so he needed only 40 yards in the regular-season finale to get 1,000 and the record.

On the first play, Tom Brady threw a 12-yard pass to Evans, and on the next drive, he added a 14-yard catch and then another for 20, giving him 1,006 and the record all to himself. And before that could even be celebrated, on the next play, Brady again looked for Evans in the end zone.

And cruelly, Evans leg slipped on the turf and he hyperextended his left knee. Trainers attended to him on the field, and as he tried to put weight on his leg, he initially couldn't. He limped off the field, and there was a real fear that he would miss the playoff opener he'd waited his entire career to play in.

But incredibly, an MRI exam showed no damage to the knee, and after barely practicing all week, he not only dressed for the wild-card game at Washington, he led the

Mike Evans made history during the 2020 campaign, becoming the first player in NFL history to begin his career with seven consecutive 1,000-yard seasons.

way, catching six passes for a game-high 119 yards in the Bucs' 31-23 win. He would add a touchdown in the win at New Orleans and another in the win at Green Bay, clinching an improbable spot in the Super Bowl.

Evans had a microphone on him for the Packers game, and it caught a genuine moment as the game ended, and he started walking toward the tunnel at the Bucs' locker room. He was stopped and told there was a ceremony on the field, with the presentation of the George Halas Trophy to the NFC champions.

"It's a ceremony?" he asked, unsure for a second. "I'm new at this, man."

Evans had much to celebrate in 2020 — on the field, he caught 13 touchdowns in the regular season, breaking the team record he had held with 12 touchdowns in 2014 and 2016. The Pro Football Hall of Fame took the jersey and gloves he wore when he got to 1,000 yards for display in Canton, and after getting that record, the congratulations he got included two of his favorite players, Dwyane Wade and LeBron James.

"I got a lot of love from a lot of my family, my friends and people that I care about, a lot of people that I look up to — D. Wade, LeBron and guys like that," said Evans, a huge NBA fan with a basketball background himself. "That's awesome — I'll never be too big to not appreciate that. Some of my childhood heroes and they're paying homage and showing love to me. It means a lot. Randy — he didn't reach out to me this time, but last year he did. He doesn't have to. I know Randy — he's a great guy, a hell of a player and one of the best to ever do it. It is an awesome record and I'm proud of it."

Evans also found a special bond with Brady as a short-yardage red-zone threat, with nine of his touchdown catches covering nine yards or less. None of that mattered as much as his team making the playoffs.

"Mike is all about winning," Arians said in December. "I've been around a lot of great receivers — can't say I've ever been around one as unselfish as he is.

He just wants to win. Obviously, he's played really hurt. A couple ballgames, he had no business being out there, but I couldn't get him off the field. I had to fight him to get him off the field."

Off the field, Evans was the Bucs' nominee for the Walter Payton Man of the Year Award, perhaps the best character accolade a player can be honored with. Evans and his wife Ashli have the Mike Evans Family Foundation, whose two purposes are to help families that have dealt with domestic violence, and to help high school students find their way to college.

"I'm humbled to be considered for such a prestigious award," Evans said. "There are so many NFL players and athletes who pay it forward and are committed to making a difference in their communities — I'm just proud to do my part." ∎

Mike Evans put up another big season receiving for the Bucs but more importantly, helped lead the team to the playoffs for the first time in his career.

NFC WILD CARD PLAYOFF

BUCCANEERS 31, WASHINGTON FOOTBALL TEAM 23
January 9, 2021 • Landover, Maryland

SURVIVE AND ADVANCE

Tampa Bay Dismisses Frisky Washington, Advances to Divisional Round

By Greg Auman

By winning the last four games of the regular season, the Bucs locked up a seed as the highest of three wild cards in the NFC playoffs, and as a result, a favorable opening draw, traveling to NFC East champion Washington, which had finished 7-9.

Facing a playoff opponent with a losing record is rare, but Tampa Bay still found a formidable opponent, with a tough defense and surprisingly strong play from the team's fourth quarterback, Taylor Heinicke, who stepped in and challenged the Bucs right to the very end.

This was not a pretty win, as the Bucs went 1-for-5 in the red zone, settling for field goals that kept Washington in the game. Coach Bruce Arians said his defense was "terrible" until the final minutes of the game, but Tampa Bay survived and advanced, and in the playoffs, that matters infinitely more than style points.

"We didn't play our best game, but at this point of the year a win's a win, so we're pretty fired up about that," said tight end Cameron Brate, who stepped up with a season-best 80 receiving yards. "We're thrilled with the win. I hate to say that we're relieved, but at this point, we're just pumped that we got the win. No matter how ugly it was, no how many mistakes we made, it doesn't matter."

The game's biggest storyline entering the week had been Redskins rookie pass-rusher Chase Young, who had come off the field after a clinching win the week before, shouting "Tom Brady! I'm coming! I want Tom!" That message was heard loud and clear by a Bucs offensive line that had protected their 43-year-old quarterback well, holding opponents to 22 sacks in 16 games.

Washington's strength was its defensive front, having held seven straight opponents to 20 points or less, but the Bucs defense — playing without inside linebacker Devin White, who had tested positive for COVID-19 a week earlier — showed up early as well. Washington went three-and-out on its first drive, and cornerback Sean Murphy-Bunting's interception set up a touchdown pass from Tom Brady to receiver Antonio Brown for a 9-0 lead (the extra point was blocked).

Heinicke, filling in with veterans Alex Smith and Kyle Allen injured and former first-round pick Dwayne Haskins recently waived, led Washington on a 75-yard touchdown drive, but the Bucs answered with a Brady touchdown to Chris Godwin, leading 18-7 at halftime.

Running back Ke'Shawn Vaughn and the Bucs hurdled Washington on their way to the Wild Card win, the team's first playoff victory since they won Super Bowl XXXVII.

Washington, which had dropped its Redskins mascot before the season and was simply the Football Team, wasn't going away, adding a field goal in the third quarter, then getting a Heinicke rushing touchdown to pull within two points. The conversion failed, and the Bucs were clinging to an 18-16 lead in the fourth quarter on the road.

Brady and the Bucs offense responded, first with a field goal, then passes of 20 and 19 yards to receiver Mike Evans to set up a 3-yard touchdown by running back Leonard Fournette, for a 28-16 lead. Evans had hyperextended his knee just six days earlier, a scary injury that had looked like something that could end his season, but tests came back negative and he made it back, not wanting to miss his first career playoff game in seven years in the NFL. Fournette, who had been a healthy scratch just four weeks earlier, shined as a starter with Ronald Jones out with a quad injury, rushing for 93 yards and adding another 39 receiving.

Heinicke had another 75-yard touchdown drive, again pulling Washington within five points, and after a fourth Ryan Succop field goal put the Bucs up eight, the Football Team still had a chance with 2:49 left to tie the game with a touchdown and two-point conversion.

Washington completed two quick passes and was across midfield when the Bucs defense stepped up to seal the win. After two incompletions, Heinicke was sacked by linebacker Lavonte David — playing in his first career playoff game in his ninth season with the Bucs — and a fourth-and-21 desperation heave fell incomplete. The Bucs had their first playoff win in nearly 18 years, since their Super Bowl win after the 2002 season.

"You could win 100-0 and it's going to be the same result in the end," Brady said of the underwhelming victory. "You'd love to play great every game — I think it's good to win and advance."

Tampa Bay's offensive line had risen to the challenge, especially tackles Donovan Smith and

Washington and quarterback Taylor Heinicke put up a good fight, but the Bucs found a way to win, propelling them to an unforgettable playoff run.

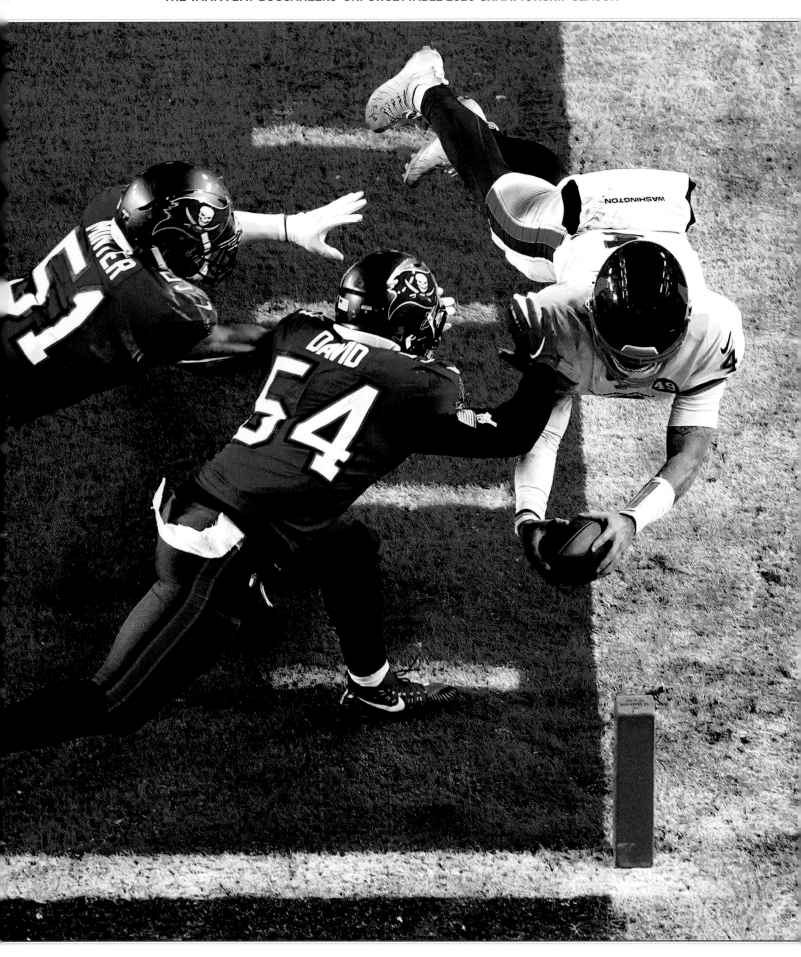

Tristan Wirfs, who held Young to no sacks, no quarterback hits and just three tackles. Brady was sacked twice, but had enough time to throw for 381 yards, easily a Bucs playoff record.

"I think it was the biggest storyline of the week, just because one guy says, 'I want Tom' all of a sudden," Arians said of his offensive line. "They've got a great front. Our guys took it to heart — they were going to block them. I thought we blocked them really, really well. They didn't scare us."

And while the defense got a stop at the end to clinch the win, they gave up 375 yards of offense to a backup quarterback making his second career start, so there was a keen awareness that they'd have to play much better with Pro Bowl quarterbacks ahead.

"I felt like we didn't make a lot of plays we should have made," Murphy-Bunting said. "There were a lot of plays we left out on the field. At the end of the day, it's a team effort, a defense effort. It takes every position, takes every player to buy in and know that what they do affects the guy next to them and so on. (Playing like that) there's no way we can go into next week's game, no matter who it is, and expect to come out with a victory. … It needs to change now." ■

Mike Evans came back from an injury scare in the last regular season game to catch six passes for 119 yards in the win over Washington.

NFC DIVISIONAL PLAYOFF

BUCCANEERS 30, SAINTS 20
January 17, 2021 • New Orleans, Louisiana

THIRD TIME'S THE CHARM

Tom Brady Outduels Drew Brees as Saints Advance to NFC Championship

By Greg Auman

When the Bucs went to New Orleans to face the Saints in the divisional round, much of the focus was on two things — the historic showdown between the Bucs' Tom Brady, 43, and the Saints' Drew Brees, 42, and the way the Saints had swept the Bucs decisively in two regular-season meetings.

In the end, the story was a young Bucs defense rising up and showing an innate ability to again force turnovers from a quarterback who doesn't make such mistakes often — or with so much on the line.

"We've been fighting adversity all year," said cornerback Sean Murphy-Bunting, one of three 2019 draft picks to get interceptions against Brees. "We've been battling the naysayers and those who say we can't do things. At the end of the day, we're all fighters. We like to battle. We like to give it our all. We wanted to make sure this wasn't our last one."

The last time the two teams met, it wasn't close at all, with New Orleans dominating on the way to a 31-0 halftime lead and a 38-3 win, easily the low point in the Bucs' season. Their first meeting was the season opener, with Brady playing without any preseason and throwing two interceptions, one of which was returned for a touchdown.

Again, Tampa Bay's offense had a slow start, but the defense held the Saints to two field goals early, and Murphy-Bunting's interception, returned to the 3, set up an easy touchdown from Tom Brady to Mike Evans for a 10-6 lead. The Bucs weren't the only ones with revenge on their mind, as Saints backup quarterback Jameis Winston, Tampa Bay's starter for the previous five years before Brady's arrival, came into the game on a trick play, taking a pitch on an end-around and throwing a 56-yard touchdown to receiver Tre'Quan Smith to retake the lead. Brady drove the Bucs 63 yards in the final 2:28 before halftime to salvage a field goal and a 13-13 tie at halftime.

New Orleans opened the second half strong, as Brees threw a touchdown pass on the opening drive for a 20-13 lead, but then the Bucs defense stepped up. The Saints had advanced into Bucs territory when rookie safety Antoine Winfield Jr. forced a fumble from New Orleans tight end Jared Cook, with linebacker Devin White scooping up the loose ball and returning it to the Saints' 40.

In what would be a postseason theme, the offense capitalized on the takeaway, with Brady throwing a touchdown to running back Leonard Fournette to tie the game at 20-20.

Tampa Bay linebacker Devin White (45) celebrates with his teammates after a huge fourth-quarter interception.

The defense forced a Saints punt, the Bucs added a field goal, but it was still a three-point game in the fourth quarter, Brees driving again. White, the Bucs' first-round pick from 2019, returning that day after missing two games due to a positive COVID-19 test, made another huge play, stepping in front of a pass for Alvin Kamara for another Brees interception, returning it to the Saints' 20.

"I know one thing: We might be young, but we can get after it when we've got our mind set to it," White said.

The offense again converted it into a touchdown, this time a Brady keeper for a commanding 30-20 lead with under five minutes left. Brees tried for another comeback, but his pass was tipped and intercepted by second-year safety Mike Edwards, sealing the Bucs' victory and a trip to the NFC Championship Game.

No team had ever beaten Brady three times in a season, but the Bucs' win wasn't an easy one by historical standards. Only twice in the previous 18 years had a team pulled off a playoff win against a team that had swept them in the regular season, but the Bucs had still entered the game with confidence.

"This is a different football team than that week," coach Bruce Arians said. "I tried to tell everybody that, and nobody wants to believe it. This is what we're capable of playing. Defensively, we've had some rough spots at times, but we've had some really, really good times, and this was one of the best times."

The young defense had upstaged the two future Hall of Fame quarterbacks, even their own, getting four takeaways, the three interceptions a postseason career high for Brees.

"They played incredible," said Brady, who had no turnovers and threw for two scores. "This team has been doing that all year. The defense has picked us up some weeks . . . the way the defense played today, they were spectacular."

Bucs' cornerback Sean Murphy-Bunting intercepts Drew Brees, one of three interceptions of the Saints' veteran quarterback in the Tampa Bay win.

The two quarterbacks, ranking as the top two in NFL history in career passing yards and touchdowns, have had very different careers in terms of postseason success. They met on the field after the game, talking for some time as Brady threw passes to Brees' children, and then went their separate ways. Brees' pursuit of just a second Super Bowl appearance to join his 2010 win was over, with his retirement widely expected, while Brady survived to continue his chase of a 10th Super Bowl and a seventh ring. ∎

Above: Fellow future Hall of Fame quarterbacks Drew Brees and Tom Brady speak after the Tampa Bay win, in what may have been the last game of Brees' illustrious career. Opposite: Tom Brady plunges into the end zone for one of his three touchdowns in the win, two coming through the air.

NFC CHAMPIONSHIP

BUCCANEERS 31, PACKERS 26

January 24, 2021 • Green Bay, Wisconsin

FEELING SUPER

Bucs Hang on Against Pack, Clinch First "Home Field" Super Bowl in NFL History

By Greg Auman

The Bucs call it complementary football: Offense and defense leaning on each other and winning.

"When we need help, they bail us out," outside linebacker Shaquil Barrett said. "When they need help, we bail them out. That's why we're playing so well right now."

Both sides played a key role in a 31-26 victory over the top-seeded Packers at Lambeau Field, allowing the Bucs to become the first team in NFL history to play a Super Bowl on their home field. Compared to their first win against Green Bay, it wasn't nearly as easy, but meant so much more.

"I couldn't be happier for our players. They put in so much work," coach Bruce Arians, whose team won in a stadium where they'd been 1-15 over the previous 30 years. "Our coaching staff has done such a great job. I just couldn't be any more elated for these guys and the job they put in ... It was a great team win."

Tampa Bay had handed the Packers a 38-10 loss in Tampa in Week 6, arguably their best game of the season, but three months had passed, with much more at stake. Far from home and the warmth of Tampa, it had snowed in Green Bay all morning, the temperature just 29 degrees at kickoff, after several players defiantly warmed up in short-sleeve shirts, others in shorts.

Tampa Bay's offense got the Bucs a 28-10 lead early in the third quarter, thanks to three touchdown passes from Tom Brady. And when Brady faltered down the stretch, the Bucs defense carried them the rest of the way.

The Bucs took control of the game, building an 18-point lead early in the third quarter by converting two Packers turnovers into touchdowns.

The first was Arians at his no-risk-it-no-biscuit best, calling his punt team off the field with 13 seconds left before halftime. Cornerback Sean Murphy-Bunting had intercepted an Aaron Rodgers pass with 28 seconds left, but the Bucs faced a fourth-and-4 at the Green Bay 45. Punting would all but assure a four-point lead at the half, but Arians called a timeout and sent his offense out, and Brady hit running back Leonard Fournette for the first down, stopping the clock with eight seconds left.

Speedy receiver Scotty Miller got past Packers cornerback Kevin King, and Brady found him for a 39-yard touchdown and a 21-10 halftime lead. "We didn't come here to not take chances to win the game," Arians said of the bold call.

The Bucs defense forced a fumble on the opening drive of the second half, as safety Jordan Whitehead popped the ball loose from Green Bay running back Aaron Jones, and linebacker Devin White scooped it up and returned it to the 8-yard line. Brady hit tight end Cameron Brate for a quick touchdown and a 28-10 lead.

Then the wheels came off.

Mike Evans opened up the scoring against the Packers with this 15-yard touchdown catch, one of his three receptions for 51 yards in the NFC Championship win.

Rodgers threw two touchdowns, and Brady — who had one interception total in the previous six games — threw interceptions on three straight drives. But the Bucs defense stepped up, forcing a three-and-out from the Packers after each of the last two interceptions, clinging to a 28-23 lead.

"We never budged. We never flinched at all," said outside linebacker Jason Pierre-Paul, who had two sacks. "We just played tremendous football and look where we're at. It doesn't matter how many picks Tom throws, the defense has his back. That's how we played. I feel like a group of brothers, when they sync, it's unstoppable."

After a Bucs field goal put them up by eight, Green Bay got all the way to the Tampa Bay 8-yard line, with Rodgers missing on three straight throws with just over two minutes left in the game. Needing a touchdown and two-point conversion to tie, Packers coach Matt LaFleur made a curious decision to kick a field goal, trusting his defense to get the ball back with the two-minute warning and all three timeouts. "I couldn't believe it, honestly," said Barrett, who had three sacks in the game.

Tampa Bay never gave them that chance, getting a first down on a pass-interference penalty, then another on an end-around to receiver Chris Godwin on third down, so they could run out the clock and clinch the win.

The Bucs celebrated on the field, wearing gray NFC Champion t-shirts and proudly hoisting the George Halas Trophy. They had won three straight road games — as many as Brady had won on the way to all nine of his previous Super Bowls combined — to earn the right to the ultimate home game, a Super Bowl in their own stadium, a first in the game's 55-year history.

"To go on the road and win another road playoff game is just a great achievement," Brady said. "Now, a home Super Bowl for the first time in NFL history, I think, puts a lot of cool things in perspective. Any time you're the first time doing something, it's usually a pretty

Rob Gronkowski only had one catch in the game, but it was a pivotal 29-yard rumble that caught the Packers by surprise.

good thing. Now, we've just got to go and have a great two weeks, prepare for whoever it is and be ready to go."

Three hours later, they would learn that the defending Super Bowl champion Kansas City Chiefs were coming to Tampa, a third straight playoff rematch against a team the Bucs had played that year.

"Familiarity helps," Arians would say the next day of another familiar opponent. "I'm not really excited to play Tyreek Hill, (Travis) Kelce and (Patrick) Mahomes. That's a formidable challenge, but our guys will be up for it." ∎

Above: Tom Brady and the Bucs won at Lambeau Field for only the second time in the last 17 tries for Tampa Bay. Opposite: Tom Brady uncorks a 39-yard touchdown to wide receiver Scotty Miller to end the first half, shocking the Packers and taking control of the game for the Buccaneers.